BECOMING UNBREAKABLE

GLEN PEARSON

PEARSON

Dedicated to the fine staff, board, volunteers and residents of St. Joseph's Hospice. And to David Nash, whose inspiring example as a friend and board chair invited my involvement and empowered my life even further.

There is no safe investment. To love at all is to be vulnerable. Love anything, and your heart will certainly be wrung and possibly be broken. If you want to make sure of keeping it intact, you must give your heart to no one, not even to an animal. Wrap it carefully round with hobbies and little luxuries; avoid all entanglements; lock it up safe in the casket or coffin of your selfishness. But in that casket – safe, dark, motionless, airless - it will change. It will not be broken; it will become unbreakable, impenetrable, irredeemable. The alternative to tragedy, or at least the risk of tragedy, is damnation. The only place outside Heaven where you can be perfectly safe from all the dangers and pertubations of love is Hell.

… C. S. Lewis

1

She sighed when the old stone structure came into view, as her car exited a grouping of trees and pulled up the small stone path to the front door.

She fumbled with the keys to the small stone cottage until, at last, she twisted the largest of them and watched as the door swung open. It consisted of heavy oak planks affixed to iron bands and, because it wasn't hung correctly in the beginning, it simply opened and noisily banged against the wall if it wasn't restrained.

Scarlett listened to the ungraceful collision between wood and stone and, smiling to herself at the novelty of it all, moved inside to the kitchen and placed the groceries on the table. She returned to the car and gathered the two bottles of red wine she had left in the front seat. Cradling them in her left arm, she used her right arm to swing the great door back into place.

"They'll wait for a few minutes," she said out loud as she eyed the grocery bags. She then opened one of the bottles and poured some of the red liquid into a large wine glass. Kicking off her shoes, she padded barefoot into the main sitting room and sank down into the deep cushions of the sofa.

Scarlett wasn't displeased as she let her gaze follow the contours of the walls and windows of the cottage's main room. Pulling her feet up beneath her while rubbing the arches, she thanked her stars once more that she had pressed the board of the parish to permit her to stay in the abandoned stone cottage instead of the two-bedroom condominium the Church of England owned in nearby Whitfield – a stone's throw from Dover and its famous white cliffs.

Ten years ago, the parish had embarked on a bold idea that was destined to stabilize its finances and enable it to enhance its religious influence in an era where the Christian faith was on the wane in most of the English countryside. With the nation's greying population growing at such a rate that care for seniors was placing great strain on Britain's vaunted (and free) healthcare system, the leader of the parish council conceived an idea. During a casual coffee with the local MP, he offered that it might be innovative to have the parish manage an end-of-life hospice if the national government would be willing to put up funds for its construction. The politician, a former architect, immediately took to the idea and called together an assembly of local leaders to discuss the possibilities and impacts.

The initiative became a welcome relief from all the Brexit brouhaha that had plunged British life into a new era of uncertainty. This was something local and perhaps meaningful. For the national government, it was an opportunity to show off its more caring side. Within a year four million pounds were allocated for the hospice's construction. Using a local builder, the planners somehow refrained from taking the easier route of erecting a modern building that would surely have been incongruous in such a setting. Instead, they opted to design an estate-like structure that utilized local wood along with limestone from the same quarry that had supplied material for the church, the parish hall, and Scarlett's cottage.

The result was a cultural and spiritual tour de force. It looked like it had been there for centuries, the builders having somehow coloured the stone to make it look older. From every angle it inspired. As little damage as possible was done to the landscape, leaving copious amounts of hardwood trees and bushes to frame the setting. The roof was made of slate shingles, covering five steeply pitched arches that settled comfortably like a favourite coat over the structure beneath.

As with everything else, the cost overruns were excessive. When it was feared that the project might falter or even remain unfinished, the residents of Whitfield and nearby Dover designed fundraisers to make up the shortfall. Sensing its popularity with the locals, the Archbishop of Canterbury instructed that special offerings for the project be taken by the various Church of England congregations throughout the south of the country.

It was enough, and though the building was six months late in completion, it was fully paid for. Upon its opening, it became the cover story for numerous magazines and periodicals, all praising the care taken in its design and construction. It was considered a tribute to community creativity, as well as an example of foresight on the part of the parish that had moved ahead with it.

But there was another key reason behind the success.

Hospices were becoming increasingly popular, especially for the wealthy seniors that had settled near the famous white cliffs for their sunset years. The entire region had become a haven for those seeking warmer winds, the company of others and, above all, the view of the English Channel that held such a sacred place of honour and history in their memories.

Though senior's residences were everywhere in the region, those entering their final months and days on earth had little choice but to pass them in bustling hospitals. Palliative care wings, for all their good intentions, were caught in the updraft of modern hospital life with all its complexities and interventions. For those wishing a more peaceful and serene setting, a hospice offered an intriguing alternative.

The government of the day also benefitted from the arrangement. Costs for treating someone near the end of life were far more extensive in a professional hospital facility. A hospice, however, founded much of its care on family members and volunteers, thereby decreasing costs while, at the same time, offering more intimate care.

The opening day had taken place eighteen months earlier, with a crowd of dignitaries gathering to celebrate the unique collaboration of civil society, professional health services, and government investment. It was decided that the first executive director would be one of the elderly ministers in the parish, who had a background in health sciences and plenty of experience in the care of others.

The arrangement was doomed from the beginning. It became abundantly clear that the supervisor had little to no managerial experience of a health facility that had to subscribe to rigorous government standards. Within two months a file of volunteers and hired staff headed out the door and what was launched as an exciting new venture now hung on the precipice of dysfunction.

The decision was made to post the job, largely on Anglican digital services both in England and Canada – a country that was excelling at hospice care as its own national health costs skyrocketed due to an aging population.

Scarlett came across the posting while working as a head nurse at an end-of-life palliative care ward in a Halifax, Nova Scotia medical centre. Her own life had taken a personal downturn in the past year and she found herself surprisingly willing to take her career in an entirely different direction. And so, she applied online and was surprised to receive a quick response, with a plane ticket and the offer of an in-depth interview with the parish board. She consented, and with little personal responsibilities in Canada, boarded an Air Canada jet to Heathrow airport. She was picked up by one of the parish board members and driven directly to St. Anne's Parish Hospice in Whitfield.

The moment she saw the vaulted arches and limestone walls, Scarlett knew she wanted this job more than any other she had experienced. She was given a quick tour, which only made her want the position even more, and was eventually guided into a well-crafted board room, lined with shelves and pieces of art depicting the region around the white cliffs.

The board chair opened the session by saying that Scarlett's application was the first one they considered and that she was their preferred option, depending on how the interview went. This surprised her, especially given that she came from across the Atlantic. She said as much before they went any further.

"We have great respect for your qualifications and experience," the board chair replied. "However, the fact that you had a rich Anglican tradition went a long way to giving us peace of mind. Much has been made of the hospice and its setting, but little was said of the religious tradition that infuses both the plan and practice of the operation. It was this parish that first formulated the idea for a hospice and we wish to ensure that the spiritual roots of the venture are both respected and built upon. Your experience in palliative care, coupled with your years of service in your Halifax congregation, seemed, to us at least, a suitable fit."

For the next hour the conversation went back and forth between Scarlett and the 14 members of the council around the table. It was clear to everyone present that for all its potential, St. Anne's Parish Hospice was faltering out of the starting blocks and that only seasoned leadership could place it on the right path.

The parish priest, also called the vicar, took Scarlett to lunch as the board deliberated on her suitability.

The Reverend Thomas Spelling could only partially contain, beneath his ecclesiastical demeanour, his excitement at Scarlett's presence. Extremely tall, slim, and with waves of unruly grey hair, Spelling had been with the parish for nearly a decade and had proved a powerful force in getting the hospice from the drafting board to its opening day. His accent was of upper-class descent but his sense of humour provided him with a gracious kind of commonality that made him a favourite with the people of the area.

"We were pretty excited about your interest in the post, you know," he said offhandedly, as they began eating their tea and sandwiches at a local deli on the main street of Whitfield.

"Yes, I'm a bit surprised at that, I must say," Scarlett responded. "I mean, you must have had plenty of interest just from within Britain."

"Not really. I suppose all that media attention would have intimidated most interested folks. Plus, the religious dimension isn't so popular these days. You seemed like an ideal fit … from a distance anyway," he concluded with a smile.

"And now that you've seen me up close?"

"Only confirms all we hoped for," the Reverend said by way of affirmation. "I told them I would have you back in an hour. Why don't we finish up and get back there?"

By mid-afternoon it was all finished. Offered the post the moment she appeared back in the boardroom, Scarlett could only reply that she hoped she was up to the task and asked that they support her as she found her way in the new position.

When she asked about accommodations, the chair noted that the parish owned a condominium in Whitfield and offered to take her to see it. He also offered to provide a tour of the parish ground. Reverend Spelling proposed he come along for the ride. A congenial bond between Scarlett and the vicar was already developing.

The drive around the parish estate was something of a revelation. Thickly wooded, with lush grass fields criss-crossed by the odd stream or brook, Scarlett took to it immediately. This was her first time in England, though she had visited Scotland years before. The drive took them to the white cliffs and the vast reach of the English Channel, made more bracing by a strong offshore breeze.

She was surprised how sparsely populated the cliff area was.

"Think of it as something like one of your national parks in Canada," the Reverend offered. "The regions around these cliffs are sacred in every way – religiously, culturally, historically, and psychologically. The threat of invasions from across the water focused the British imagination on these shorelines like little else – especially during World Two. The national government moved quickly to protect these cliffs from development since they knew they would be a natural magnet for both their beauty and property value. They look much as they did when the Spitfires and Hurricanes flew overhead in the Battle of Britain and the D-Day forces moved out across the Channel."

They drove through the parish lands on their final leg into Whitfield, where her hotel was located. It was then that she noticed the small stone cottage, nestled among some chestnut and fir trees, situated one-quarter mile from the hospice.

"What's in there?" she asked curiously.

"Nothing, really," the Reverend replied. "The roof is dilapidated, as you can see, and the door and windows have fallen into disrepair. The gardeners store some of their tools there, but little else. It is supplied with water and electricity, but the cost for renovations caused past councils to defer any decisions on it.

It was small compared to the other estate buildings and she learned that it had been the home of a succession of groundskeepers. It was clearly rundown, but its profile made it both quaint and attractive. On a whim, the board chair pulled into the short driveway that meandered by the front of the structure. Above the door, carved into a bevelled piece of chestnut wood was the word *Mulladore.*

"It's beautiful," Scarlett said in a quiet voice.

"Yes, I suppose that's most of the reason it hasn't been torn down yet," the chair replied.

Ten minutes later they pulled off of the A2 carriageway and drove up to the condominium. It was modern and looked much like the structures beside it. All the amenities were nearby and she would only be a few minutes' drive from St. Anne's.

As they began to exit the vehicle to take a tour of the inside, Scarlett asked, "Would there be any willingness on the Council's part in permitting me to stay in the stone cottage?"

It was offered so simply and directly that both men were caught off-guard.

"Why would you want to do that, Ms. Carlyle?" asked the chair. "I mean, attractive as it is, Mulladore is a run-down ruin. You'd never be comfortable there."

"I don't intend to stay here a short time," she replied. "It will take a few years to get a new organization running well and, in the meantime, I wouldn't mind working on the place myself. My father was a carpenter, you see, and I picked up a number of skills from him. I would enjoy the work and I will pay for all the materials."

Before the board chair could say anything further, Reverend Spelling said, "What a splendid idea. You'll likely require something to help you work out your emotions from St. Anne's. I know leading a hospice is exhausting work. I say: let's get the council's approval of Scarlett's request. Surely we don't have any other plans for the place?" The board chair shrugged in quiet assent.

By the time she returned from settling her affairs in Canada, Scarlett drove up the driveway to see a recently installed slate roof and repaired and painted windows. It didn't look like new, but she would never have desired that. What she saw was an ancient cottage modernized with taste and efficiency. She couldn't believe her luck.

And that's how she ended up on this sofa, caressing her red wine, and enjoying the ambience. Scarlett had spent the last few months installing new interior window and door frames. The kitchen counter had been an old chestnut plank board that had been there for decades and was cracked and deeply stained. She replaced it with off-white ceramic tiles, added a ceramic sink, and deftly caulked their perimeters with silicone.

The most laborious task was replacing the old coal stove in the kitchen with a newer wood-burning model that afforded four burners, a deep oven, and even a hot plate set off to the side for keeping the kettle warm. The fireplace flue in the living room required repairing and this she contracted out to a local masonry firm, paying in cash the moment they were finished.

Scarlett had much work left to do, but she had done what was necessary to make it livable, warm and efficient. When she offered Mulladore as a possible setting for one of St. Anne's board meetings, every member of the group came and marvelled at the transformation their new recruit had performed. Her skill at woodworking impressed even the most skeptical, leaving some to wonder why they hadn't renovated the cottage earlier.

She placed her empty wineglass on the table before her, scolding herself for not getting up and putting the perishable food in the refrigerator.

Scarlett recalled her first thought as she entered the heavy door - *I died again today and yet here I am, carting in the groceries*. It was true every day, although only those acquainted with deep grief could comprehend it. Two patients had their final passing at St. Anne's, both in the afternoon. Mary was an 87-year-old woman from outside of London who had descended deeper and deeper into Alzheimer's over the past ten years. Her final struggle ended with her family cradling her head and holding both her hands. Scarlett had been there to watch the minister deliver the Last Rites.

The second passing was that of a 37-year-old truck driver who never recovered consciousness after his semi-truck swerved to avoid a car. Unmarried, his two sisters stood as faithful sentinels to a life that mattered – at least to them. Scarlett had wept with them when the final breath was expelled. It was difficult to accept the death of a young man who perished because a drunk woman had journeyed down the wrong side of the highway.

She laid her head back on the soft arm of the sofa and quietly mumbled prayers for both. The truth was that she felt she had died every occasion when one of her hospice guests passed away. Yet, each morning that followed, she would be raised from the dead again to journey once more in the valley of death. It was grief-filled and exhausting. The fatigue of the day descended on her like a gentle sweater. She laid her head back on the soft arm of the sofa and quietly mumbled her thanks for her good fortune. The groceries would have to wait, since within a minute she was sound asleep.

2

Mulladore lay on the periphery of the parish estate. Initially it had occupied the core of St. Anne's holdings, but as the parish grew in numbers and prominence, it acquired more and more land to the west over two centuries. The church, parish halls, and the hospice were situated a good half-mile from Mulladore, leaving it more or less isolated. Eventually it was abandoned and was now the most eastern structure on the property.

Scarlett didn't mind this kind of accidental remoteness, since it provided her some space from where she worked and also some solitude, which the condominium in Whitfield would never have afforded.

There were the remnants of a small garden in the rear, with a small stone pathway winding through it. There was even an outside water faucet which she was delighted to discover still worked.

The first few weeks were taken up with renovations inside the cottage, but as they eventually were completed, Scarlett began investing her energies in fixing up the property. Painting the eaves and re-pointing the double brick chimney came first and only then did she concentrate on the grounds.

It was then that she detected the scent of Cavendish pipe tobacco in the air – the same kind her father used to smoke. She walked around the property looking for its source. It was only as she came around the front that she spotted a man working on his own garden across the road, an old briar pipe hanging precariously from his mouth. He wore dungarees and an old fisherman's hat with various kinds of fishing flies attached to its broad brim.

She was too shy to call over and he was too preoccupied to even notice her, but the next day he appeared as she worked the garden, a box of plants and bulbs cradled in his arms. She rested her hoe against a fir tree and moved towards him.

"You're my new neighbour, I suspect. My name's Bert Wynman and I thought I'd bring along some items for your garden, to get you started anyway."

She held out her hand to shake his, only to see that he didn't have a free one of his own. "Why, thank you, Bert," she said, taking the box from his grasp and placing it on a flat rock. "I'm Scarlett Carlyle. I'm sorry I haven't had the chance to do the rounds of introductions with folks here. I've been told the autumn rains spring up suddenly and I wanted to make sure the house was ship-shape before they arrive. It's kept me preoccupied. Again, sorry."

"You did all this work yourself?" he asked, clearly astonished.

"My father was a carpenter; I come by it honestly."

He smiled before saying, "Well, you know what you're

doing. I've never seen the place look so good. Kind of nice actually."

He was of average height and his darkened skin showed that he was a man comfortable in the out-of-doors. He hadn't shaved for the last two days, but it suited him. His hair was once blonde but was now thinning and losing its lustre. Scarlett pegged him to be about forty, or even a bit older.

She cast a glance over her shoulder at his gift on the rock and asked, "Why don't we have some tea or coffee? It's kind of my way of saying thanks for the plants, which I'll get started on later today.

"Well, then, I accept. Coffee would be great, actually. Nobody ever talks about it, but we Brits drink almost double the amount of coffee over tea every day. Some say it was because of all those Yanks stationed here during the war – 1,600,000 of them, something like that."

"Seriously? That many? I had no idea. That's a lot of visitors."

He smiled knowingly before saying, "They were a lot more than visitors in the end. Some died and were buried here. Others bought pubs, shops, even vehicles and opted to remain here once V.E. Day came. Of course, there were some half a million of them that sported our young women away as war brides and settled them back in the States. We were never quite the same after their presence."

"Well, you did get coffee out of it, at least," Scarlett said, eliciting a smile from him once more.

Fifteen minutes later they sat in the rustic kitchen and sipped at their coffee and nibbled on some shortbread.

Bert's seasoned eye roamed the interior, noticing everything.

"Given what you were up against, you have done a remarkable job," he said. "How did you get the window frames back in square shape? I mean, they were askew for what must have been half a century."

His host blushed slightly at the compliment. "I just did what my Dad would have done. I pulled off the entire frame, which had only been lightly nailed in place. Then I put some dowels where the pieces were joined, glued them together, and put them back up."

"Did you screw them back in instead of nailing?"

Scarlett was glad for his interest and answered, "No … I, lagged them with a masonry drill bit in the top corners and left it at that. Seems to have worked."

After a moment's silence she asked, "You seem to know a fair bit about carpentry and construction, Bert. Did you do a lot of that on your house?"

"I'm an architect by trade and designed my home from scratch, then had the materials shipped in and worked away at it. Took me almost ten months."

"What?" she asked, clearly surprised. "It doesn't look as old as this place – nothing does around here – but your place seems to have been there for decades."

She watched as his eyes filled up with pride and was glad he was pleased.

"Actually, the stone I used for the walls and chimney were from an old office in a nearby town. "The regional government had decided to tear it down and I asked if I might do the job for them. They agreed, naturally, and I took each stone apart piece by piece and had an old farmer bring all the stones back here in his wooden wagon. Only took seven trips, but he did it and I got to working on them right away."

Bert went on for the next twenty minutes about how he pieced his house back together, fashioning it to look as old as seemed proper for the area. He turned out to be a wealth of information about the region and its history.

"Are you still doing architectural work?" asked Scarlett.

"Only on rare occasions. I was fortunate in that I started my private business here, near the coast and, of course, the cliffs. The government hired me to refashion a large number of their own historic structures and that kept me going for almost twenty years. It was lucrative enough that it enabled me to retire early. Periodically they'll ask me to re-purpose one of their old scientific or radar buildings on the shore, especially with the 100th anniversary of the end of the First World War. It turns out that history can actually be quite lucrative."

They both shared a hearty laugh.

A revealing thread of discussion began with Scarlett's next question. "So, do you have family here? Children?"

Without even looking up, Bert replied simply: "No, no, nothing like that. I enjoy my freedoms – take great pleasure in them, actually. I've always viewed marriage as a kind of sentimental enclosure that eventually becomes stifling."

She looked at him, a half-smile on her face.

"What? You really believe that?"

"Well, I presume I must, since I have yet to form any lasting romantic attachments. I've enjoyed certain dalliances and discussions with remarkable women, but I've worked diligently to keep things at a distance. It's like the gardening we both do here – one must constantly weed to keep things from getting overgrown."

Scarlett sat back, dumbstruck. She poured them each a second cup and noted, "A lot of people use that analogy as a metaphor for love and marriage. You know, keep other things from getting in the way of a couple's commitment to one another?"

He accepted the cup from her. "It cuts both ways. Most of my associates either are or were married and I watch them get more and more enveloped in family responsibilities, leaving them unable to pursue other interests that once meant a lot to them."

"Men and women?"

"Both," he affirmed.

"So, you've never considered marriage?" she prodded.

"Not once."

Bert's reply was so definitive, so self-assured, that it left his host feeling slightly unsettled. She looked down at the remaining coffee in her mug.

"That disappoints you?" he asked.

She looked up quickly. "No, no. Just surprised a bit, that's all. I don't think I can ever recall meeting another person with that outlook."

"I bet you have, but you just didn't know it," he said assuredly. "The thing is that there are plenty of liberated souls out there who have come to that view, only *after* their lives of normal commitments didn't work out for them. I see it everywhere – and maybe it's just part of this modern age – but witnessing such experiences convinced me early on that I desired a life that wasn't vulnerable to such pains and surprises. And it has worked for me. I'm happy. I have a good living. And I'm not encumbered by relationships or financial commitments that tie me down to the degree where I felt trapped."

A few minutes later, she walked with him down the front path leading to the roadway. "I've disappointed you, I suspect," Bert said. "That not the best way to begin dialogue with a new neighbour and I sincerely apologize."

She waved her hand to the side in a way that implied he needn't worry. But she was somewhat unmoored by all she had heard in the last few minutes. She attempted to cover it over so her confusion wouldn't be seen.

They walked across the road together after he offered to give her a tour of his residence. It was an intriguing mix of old and modern. It was only then that she noticed that the consistency in the stones forming his house were different from those in Mulladore.

"There are different quarries all around here," he noted once she voiced the distinction. "You can always find the venerable stone cottages of England whenever a quarry is nearby. The earliest structures were made from the great oak forests that once covered the land, but once they were depleted and the price of lumber escalated beyond the reach of the average worker, stone became the easiest alternative."

She listened attentively, thankful for the change in subject but also for the history lesson she was receiving.

"Your cottage is made of the most popular stone in the area: limestone. The white cliffs off in the distance are all limestone. We're actually standing in the middle of the great limestone belt of England that runs all the way from Dorset in the southwest to Lincolnshire in the North of England. It is easy stone to work with because it's soft, almost like chalk, and shapes easily. Its smooth finish causes its hue to look different depending on the light. Though it turns grey, like your cottage, over time, it can still show some of its original honey blonde colour when bathed by the morning's rays. I've watched your place almost glow in the mornings when I look out my kitchen window.

Scarlett made a note to herself to come outside in the early hours of the day to witness the subtle phenomenon for herself.

"But the stone of your place is different," she observed.

He nodded. "Larger buildings, like many castles, government offices or churches, for whatever reason, opted for what's called Cotswold stone. It comes from more northern regions of England, was created in the Jurassic era and, as a result, is full of fossils. It was believed to be tougher but that was a fallacy. It's really limestone like that in your cottage but from a different region."

"It seems a bit lighter in hue," she noted.

"That's why I selected it. It seems to resist turning grey as quickly and is remarkably easy to work with."

They toured the rest of the grounds, concluding with Bert's invitation to see the inside of the house. But Scarlett declined.

"I'm sorry I didn't send an invite sooner," he said sheepishly. "I thought it best that we meet each other first."

"That makes sense," she responded, holding out her hand to shake his. "Thank you for the plants, Bert. Your house is so beautiful on the outside that I look forward to seeing the interior soon."

Scarlett walked through his gate and across the road, harbouring the distinct feeling that he was watching her. Once inside she began cleaning up the plates and coffee mugs and thought through their discussion over and over again. Bert Wynman was an oddity, to be sure. He was clearly a successful man of modern Britain but somehow he seemed carved out of its history. He was attractively rustic in appearance and clearly self-sufficient. But it was this last point that befuddled her. He seemed more self-contained that anyone she had ever met.

She found herself wondering if he was attracted to her. They were roughly the same age, both successful and fit. But she was single because of one of life's harsher realities, whereas he was everything he was by choice – an island unto himself and somehow cold as a result, despite his congenial nature.

She finished up, walked outside, and began the process of planting the bulbs and plants he had given her. Scarlett refused to stare at the house across the road, but she couldn't help but wonder if he was still watching her.

3

Scarlett dipped her head and sobbed. That was one of those strange things about working with those who were ending the final days of life. You always hear about those who grow used to tragedy, even immune to its reach and how it is used, consciously or not, as a coping mechanism to deal with life's most urgent moments. But Scarlett had learned early that this rarely happened in a hospice.

Perhaps it was because the end-of-life drama is more like a family movement in a place like this – not a lone soul struggling in its final steps, but a gathering of intimates that each brought their own sense of hope, grief, memory, and loss to the pageant of death. Or maybe it was the fact that St. Anne's, like pretty well every other hospice, is largely filled with volunteers who were not only there for a reason, but because most of them had been through this process, becoming empowered, seasoned, and evidencing more human capacity as a result. The hospice structure itself swelled with such human potential.

Scarlett had once heard a message where someone

quoted something from Martin Luther during the Reformation: "Every man must do two things alone; he must do his own believing and his own dying." Scarlett now understood that this wasn't true. Every death in this place was a shared play, with a cast of characters brim full of memories and history. Those final moments of breath and heartbeat were shared by everyone at their loved one's side. In fact, it was that knowledge that gave the person passing on a sense of purpose, of history, of *companionship*. They were likely never more covered in love and affection than in those moments.

Scarlett's tears this morning came as a result of watching one of these great passion plays unfold in its final few hours. She didn't try to fend off those memories, understanding that, in embracing them, she would come out the other side stronger for what she had witnessed.

Sandi Templeton had been a children's entertainer over the course of her career, in both public appearances and, later, a television program. Loved by millions, many Brits over 60 grew up with Templeton in their formative years. She had retired a decade ago and did what she always wanted to do – move to the white cliffs and cultivate her own garden. Her privacy respected by the locals, she was living her dream when she was suddenly taken down by esophageal cancer. It struck quickly and hard. It was only four months from the time she was diagnosed until she was placed in St. Anne's hospice.

News of her final struggle became commonplace after a BBC One special was in the works about her long-lasting influence on entire generations of children. Letters, emails, gifts, and old photos poured into the hospice in the days immediately after the news had broken. Sandi Templeton had been an innate part of millions of families' journeys over the years, and the affection that was felt for her, especially with her end imminent, was overwhelming.

Templeton was living by the seaside with her husband, and her two older daughters came to visit them regularly. Now, they merely shifted their ministrations and affections a few miles up the carriageway to Whitfield and St. Anne's.

Scarlett had seen such familial devotion before, but never played out on such a wide tapestry. Prior to losing consciousness, Sandi had attempted to read the cards and letters sent to her by the thousands. But she could never keep up with the deluge of well-wishes, leaving her husband, two daughters, and some hospice volunteers to read to her what they could. At some point, Scarlett came to realize that in all of her years of care she had never witnessed grief and compassion on such a grand scale.

Now, in her office, with her head in her hands, she fell into the comfort of the remarkable grief of it all – a comfort because only death itself, seen like this, could turn grief into one of the inspiring aspects of life. She lifted her eyes to examine the quote hanging on her wall and understood just how remarkably true and durable it was:

*Death is not the opposite of life, but an
ennobling part of it.*

A knock on the door caused her to quickly arrange her bangs and wipe the tears away. A respectful moment later, the form of Delores Pampau, the head duty nurse, stood in the doorway.

"Just seeing how you are, Scarlett," she said quietly. "That was a tough one."

"Indeed." Suddenly she felt choked up again and opted to remain silent.

"The folks from the funeral home just called and said that the arrangements for Sandi's funeral went smoothly enough. Apparently, the daughters bore well through all those details."

Scarlett thought back to what had just occurred two hours earlier, when Sandi had breathed her last. The resident doctor phoned the coroner, who arrived quickly and confirmed the time of death. And then began one of the most mystical and powerful customs practiced at St. Anne's. A Scottish quilt that Sandi loved was placed over her entire body and then the stretcher was reverently rolled out into the main atrium. And in a ceremony well-practiced by the people in the hospice – professionals, volunteers, and remaining patients – the resident chaplain, in this case a Roman Catholic priest, stood at the head of the stretcher and offered praise for the woman's remarkable life and prayers for the family. Then the stretcher was wheeled through the gathered crowd, with many reaching out to touch the form as if she were still alive.

It was a routine that happened almost every time someone passed, but Sandi's case was different because *she* was different. Perhaps it was her entertainer past, but she had the ability to express her emotions with no filters, no airs. She was aware of her marvellous life through it all, but there was little doubt that she also knew that many were struggling with the news that she was in her final weeks.

So, she had remained positive, even permitting an interview with a woman's magazine during her first few days in the hospice.

Sandi Templeton was the best-known person to ever be in St. Anne's, but in her own way she was just like everyone else – fighting through moments when her body was betraying her, being flooded with memories of family, friends, and career, and ultimately facing the inevitable and finding the grace to do it well.

But, as with any profound human drama, it was exhausting to both watch and care for. This was a unique and poignant day for St. Anne's, a moment in time that they were all to remember. Scarlett was still mulling it over when the voice of her head nurse had broken in on her reflections.

"Do you want me to get everyone started and give you a bit more time?"

Scarlett suddenly realized that she had forgotten the regular staff meeting, always held on the first Friday of the month following the close of the day shift – a session that served as both a business and reflective opportunity at the end of the week. She silently chastised herself for her forgetfulness, then sighed, realizing that a day such as this was likely throwing everyone off their balance.

"No, no, I'll be there in a minute. The food ready?"

"All set," Delores answered. "See you in a bit."

The door's special hinges permitted it to shut silently, leaving Scarlett undisturbed for just another minute. After placing a tissue to her eyes, she rose, grabbed a folder and pen, and headed down to the small conference room.

She opened the door to distinct sounds of sobbing and voiced condolences. Staff and volunteers alike were still attempting to deal with Sandi's loss and the moving moments that followed. Delores was already moving around the room – a hug here, and encouraging word there. Scarlett felt too exhausted to follow her example and wearily made her way to the single chair and table that faced the rest of the room.

She realized there was no point in pursuing any kind of agenda. The pain was too great, the memory too fresh. She opted to do what any good supervisor would do and encouraged them to voice what they were feeling, to comfort one another in their collective sadness.

And that's just what they did. The most popular memories centered around Sandi's sense of humour, but there were other moving comments about her acceptance of her fate or how she had spent the last weeks helping her family to deal with the grieving process even before the end.

Their boss played no part in this movement of human emotion, but only marvelled at how fortunate she was to have a staff and some senior volunteers who remained so deeply committed to humanity. She spotted Delores staring at her with a look that implied she should say a few words to draw all the threads together. Scarlett was surprised to note that it was something she really wanted to do.

"This will be a day we will long remember," she began – words that caused everyone to look up in expectation. "We've learned today that our grieving is scalable to the lives we lose. We are going to hurt for a long time, but it will be a beautiful hurt because Sandi's was a remarkably beautiful life."

Scarlett paused a moment, fighting the tears that threatened to emerge with every vowel, every syllable.

"We are supposed to be professionals but, really, there is

no such thing in this line of work – only differing levels of experience, of hearts shaped by pain and our own vulnerabilities to those we serve. We've seen so much, endured too much, learned so very much.

"Over time, we have come to regard death itself as a gift, a guest in some way. We understand what would happen if it didn't come. The pain, sadness, and wasting away of human flesh and spirit would merely go on in unendurable fashion, and we would be charged with watching over the decline. But as Sandi's remarkable time with us has revealed, through hospice care we have, instead, been given the privilege of watching over movements towards death that are often as majestic and hopeful as anything else we encounter in life.

"It just that … that…" She stopped mid-sentence and everyone understood why, as tears were more than plentiful in that moment. Scarlett gathered her wits about her and continued. "It's just that it's so damned hard on us at the same time. We're exhausted and our emotions are spent. I could try to capture this moment for some inspiring thought to encourage you all, but what's the point. You are likely stronger than I am and you've certainly done more that I have in Sandi's final days. You don't so much need encouragement as you need rest. You need to go home to your special others and weep with them. Let's just end this meeting here instead of going on with our usual business. I'm so proud of all of you, and that's not just a phrase. I watched you guide Sandi across the threshold to a new world today, and you gave her family the assurance that the new place is a better place. Get some rest. Restore your souls. See you on Monday."

By the time she crossed the threshold at Mulladore, she

was completely spent of energy or strength. Scarlett dragged herself to the couch, tossed off her shoes, and opened a vodka cooler, which she downed quickly. She opened another and felt the slight blurring around the edges of her consciousness that signalled the alcohol was having its desired effect.

Death had gotten the better of her today. But so had hope. Her emotions had ricocheted between the two realities, leaving her fatigued. Despite it all, she was pleased to discover that she sensed fulfillment, even as she felt empty. Such were the dualities and ironies of hospice work. Life and death, pain and release, joy and sadness, glory and grief, temporal and eternal, company and solitude – these had become her steady companions on her ongoing path of service.

Scarlett recalled something her father had once mentioned: Do not fear death so much but rather the inadequate life. She realized once more that, in following his counsel, she had encountered a full life. He had been correct – something she celebrated over and over again in her life.

She spotted the television channel changer on the side table a few feet away and deliberated whether to get up to reach it. Instead, she downed the last of her second cooler and drifted off into a welcome oblivion, her long limbs sprawled across the couch.

4

───────

They seemed like little fairies, thousands of them, floating through the air, and their presence drew out and eventually lifted her spirit. They were merely particles of dust, disturbed by the movement of people in the sanctuary and illuminated by the morning rays of the sun slanting in through the arched stained-glass windows. But they were beautiful and non-threatening and somehow filled the air with a kind of stillness – suitable for a setting where the soul was to engage its Maker.

Scarlett had woken with a start, thinking she had slept in and was late for work. Sandi Templeton's passing had worked its complex path through her emotions yesterday – Saturday – and she chose to deal with it by working in Mulladore's garden. The effort had exhausted her and by the end of the day, her arm and leg muscles, labouring with the beginnings of stiffness, gave up in protest. She drew a bath and soaked for an hour, delighting in a glass of red wine and some old cheddar she had purchased in the market. She had fallen into bed and enjoyed a dreamless sleep.

As the realization that it was Sunday morning permeated her consciousness, she laid her head back on the pillow and gently stretched her arms in an effort to overcome the slight pain from the activities in the garden.

Now, as she sat in a pew halfway up the aisle, she enjoyed the morning light as it filtered its way gracefully through the windows, playing its colours on the floor and walls in a kind of symphony of iridescence. They drew her gaze into the corners and nooks of the quaint sanctuary and assisted her spirit in healing following the rigours of the week just past.

St. Anne's church was beguiling and simple. From the outside, situated on the banks of the River Allen, it appeared like a cathedral in miniature – soaring steeple, thin arched windows, a steep roof, and even a graveyard to its side. But once inside, the perspective changed and one felt comfortably nestled in a quaint chapel that drew the eyes everywhere. The outside was majestic but the interior intimate – a wonderful and inspiring mix.

She had come gently into the setting with a spirit of quiet anticipation. Scarlett had spoken over the garden wall yesterday to Bert Wynman, who had reminded her that he had promised her dinner and wondered if the next day would work. She had agreed and now felt thankful that she didn't have to prepare her own dinner. And she was eager to see how her neighbour, being an architect, had constructed his home.

But the sense of longing at this moment, as she sat in the pew and waited for the service to commence, was one of spiritual expectation. Her Anglican roots and the way her parents had remained devoted to that heritage had lingered with her, even now following their deaths a number of years ago.

But her spirit and mind had expanded, opened even, since those earlier years. For her, God had become more universal and limitless. Unlike others her age, however, Scarlett never wandered off into the field of individual spirituality that left one isolated from institutional religion. She had worked her larger life out within the context of the church and had been comforted by its abiding presence and tolerance of her quest for meaning.

Almost silently, a door opened at the west side of the narthex, and the tall lean figure of Reverend Thomas Spelling almost glided his way in front of the choir before seating himself on a single wooden bench close to the lectern. He seemed built for dignity, his grey hair resting on his priestly collar and his posture erect but casual. The vicar permitted his eyes to scan the congregation and he provided the briefest of recognition to Scarlett as his gaze moved about.

The choir began its call to worship as everyone drew to attention. The church was roughly two-thirds full, as, with many such structures in England, attendance had waned in recent decades and the threat of irrelevance was never far from conscious thought.

Scarlett's mind went through the routine of Anglican worship as though it was second nature, which, she supposed, it was. Then came her favourite aspect of the service: Spelling's sermon. Sometimes he would speak for fifteen minutes in a conversational style that nevertheless carried authority with it. On other occasions, he split his message between the sermon and the homily he delivered during the weekly mass. Scarlett appreciated the former, since it allowed her to concentrate his reasonings without being distracted.

On this morning, Spelling's lilting baritone voice carried the message of openness.

> *"Since the inception of the church all those centuries ago, its leaders have depended on Christianity's mystery, its penchant for secrecy, to maintain their control over their flocks. It now seems an entirely dubious exercise in a world of the Internet and personal liberation. Religion's validity was to be discovered in its open simplicity. We are to love, to forgive, to gather, and to heal our world – nothing secret about such things. Is a woman hungry? Then give her bread. Is a child in need of an education? Then give it. Does someone require a cup of cold water, or a cloak, or shorts? Then give them, all in the name of Christ. It was a message so simple that it could empower the smallest child to the wisest elder. But that meant that leaders weren't as essential for a soul to live its life in the grace of God. And so, the mystery of the mass, the understanding of the scriptures, the vision needed for the future – all these were magnified so as to strengthen the hold of the religious elites so that they might keep their power. Simplicity was transcended by complexity, and the great*

> *gospel of love of Jesus Christ never*
> *recovered from that transformation."*

Thoughts and reasonings such as these would have been wholly out of place even a few decades ago, but the traditional church was changing, ably led by people like Spelling, who, despite his age, was at the forefront of a new kind of transcendent Christianity. The question was: would it change in time to rescue itself from oblivion and redundancy?

While others drifted downstairs for tea and biscuits following the service, Scarlett made her way down the main aisle to make her way back outside. Spelling was there, shaking hands and conferring grace. When he saw her, the vicar motioned for her to wait briefly as he finished his greetings with those gathered around him.

"I heard about Friday and Sandi Templeton's passing," he said quietly as he motioned her to the edge of the narrow narthex. "Must have been difficult."

Scarlett smiled weakly. "Tough it was, but that's why I come here every Sunday. Your messages continue to counteract the hardships that keep coming our way at St. Anne's Hospice. Thank you for that, Thomas."

She was one of the few people who called him by his first name. But then again, others didn't work as closely with the vicar in such difficult circumstances. The hospice was one of those places on his rounds each week, and his place on the board proved to be a helpful resource.

"I just want to assure myself that you are alright," the minister said sincerely. "I know the emotional price of such things. Even we in the clergy crash every now and then as we are thrust into the maelstrom of death, often barely hanging onto stability ourselves, even as we seek to guide others through the valley of the shadow."

He placed his hand on her shoulder and let it linger in consolation. "It is important that we keep our champions functioning, Scarlett, and you are clearly one of them — especially for those of us in St. Anne's. Why don't we try for a lunch in the next couple of weeks? I discovered a fabulous cheese bistro in Dover last month. You'd enjoy it."

"Thank you, Vicar," she replied formally. "I'd like that. Let's talk about it the next time you're doing your rounds."

They shook hands one final time before she exited through the side narthex oak door, pulling her collar up over her exposed neck and throat in an effort to fend off the chilly wind blowing up from the Channel. Spelling's challenge of making faith simpler and more universal continued to filter through her mind on the brief walk back to Mulladore.

A few hours later, following a pleasurable afternoon nap, she was standing at Bert Wynman's threshold, her arms full of a bottle of red wine, a basket of flowers from the market, and some Balderston cheese.

"You needn't bring the wine with you," he genially said as he ushered her into the entranceway. "I have plenty of good stuff here. But the cheese? I could definitely do with some of that."

The both laughed lightly as he took the wine from her and led Scarlett into the kitchen. Her eyes took in the vaulted ceiling, supported by crafted beams that seemed to come out of some ancient chapel. Catching her gaze, Wynman noted, "They're from the old train station that straddled the tracks in Swingate for over two centuries. When asked by the government to design a more modern and efficient version, I agreed on the condition that I keep some of the important timbers in the old edifice. They're made of oak, and at their age they are as hard as rock. I had a difficult time shaping them to the contours of this more confined space, but the effort was worth it. I love it in here."

The words were said so respectfully, so fondly, that a broad smile crossed his guest's face.

"They're beautiful – nothing like anything I've ever seen in a kitchen." He grinned pleasurably in return and held out a glass of wine for her.

"Come, let me show you around," he said, moving deeper into the house.

For the next twenty minutes they toured the various rooms, each with its own uniqueness and, she noted, with its own very English feel. She knew his pride in the home was important to him so she continued to ask questions about the construction and design, as opposed to the furniture or wall colours. Wynman picked up on her efforts immediately and relished explaining the process and thinking that went into the design of each location.

Eventually they ended back at the kitchen. Her host explained that he didn't bother with a dining room, since he lived alone, but constructed a long nook overlooking the garden and that contained a six-foot long dining table and four chairs.

"The original plan was for a dining area," he explained, "but I decided I could use the space to build a larger library and planning area instead."

"*Planning* area?"

"For my architectural specs," he answered. "Architectural drafts take up a lot of room, especially when so much detail goes into each plan. It just made sense to use the room as a professional area as opposed to a dining place that I would never have used anyway."

"So, we're eating here then," she observed, looking down at the table.

"Actually, no," he replied with a pleasant smile. "For tonight I've cooked up some cheese fondue. I'll pour the cheese into that special pot there and we can carry it through to the living room, in front of the fire."

Scarlett hadn't tasted fondue for years. She helped by carrying in the forks and basket of bread. Her host placed the cheese pot on the table and journeyed back to the kitchen to fetch the wine.

Owing to the fire, the room was a bit too warm, but she didn't mind. Both had to keep putting the pieces of crusty bread on the tongs of their forks, mixing them in the cheese so that it wouldn't burn. It tasted wonderful.

"So, how was church today?" Bert asked. When he saw her look at him in a manner that wondered how he knew, he added, "I saw you walk to the road and thought you looked rather smart. It was about time for the morning service at St. Anne's, so I just presumed that's where you were headed."

"Well, you presumed correctly," she chimed in.

"And how's old Reverend Tom?" he asked with an impish grin. "We go way back."

"Well, I know him as both my vicar and from the board of the hospice. I find him kind and insightful on both counts. "

Bert drew back into his chair and gave her an appraising look. "I thought about that connection today — between your work and your church, I mean. I can see how both require each other. You've got a hard job and I don't envy you."

It was the most insightful thing he had said in their brief relationship, and she found it touching.

"Surprised?" he asked, his left eyebrow raised in comic fashion.

"A bit, yes. I seem to recall you saying you liked keeping aloof from attachments. Maybe I had that wrong."

He smiled and rose to reach over and fill her wine glass. "I *am* human, you know. I just don't take to a complicated life. I like fashioning my own things and not having to depend on anything, or anyone, more than necessary. But the hospice? It's the kind of work that transcends everything temporal. And from what I hear, you have made quite a mark there."

None of this was what Scarlett had expected. She had thought him to be accomplished, slightly judgmental, and above all aloof. He was now proving to be quite the opposite. In Bert she had found an intelligent and compassionate neighbour which, given her line of work, was about as good as she could expect.

The dinner continued, accompanied by more wine and stimulating discussion. She learned of his background, where he was educated, and the early beginnings of his architectural training. Yet she noticed that he carefully steered away from anything that spoke of human emotion. How he *felt* about things was rarely mentioned. She decided to probe further.

"In my time here, I have never seen you at church, even though you say you and Tom know each other well," she observed.

"Our interactions are more like those of sparring partners," he noted with a tinge of humour. "I suppose you could say we have consolidated our relationship as friends, but we have learned it's best just to keep away from religious talk. It's not for me and he is kind enough to keep things that way. But I have great respect for the humanity in this man and how he cares for people. He's a truly dignified gentleman – the kind you don't see as much anymore."

Scarlett reviewed every aspect of their discussion after walking across the road to Mulladore. She had enjoyed it all, and Bert had proved to be an adept and genial host. Yet she came away, as she had previously, with the impression that something was missing. He was pleasant company and attentive to her interests, but at some level that human connection she was always seeking just wasn't there. That same humanity her neighbour respected in her vicar was somehow remote, or not even present, in him. It would be a subject she would return to over and over in her mind in the days to come.

5

Her back was turned when Thomas Spelling entered the hospice library and reflection room. Scarlett was a wonder, he realized once again. In the five months she had been at St. Anne's, there had been a noticeable change in the direction and tenor of the organization. Where there had been confusion and staff struggles since the inception, there was now the abiding sense that the hospice had quietly assumed its place in the hearts of those in the region, including in Dover, Canterbury, and as far away as Hastings. Part of it was the notoriety the hospice had received with the passing of the nationally loved Sandi Templeton. A multitude of media stories had, for a brief time, placed St. Anne's at the centre of public interest. But that had passed and now the hospice had become as sentimentally favoured as the Parish Hall or even the favourite central garden in Whitfield.

And it was due to the remarkable woman before him, the vicar knew. Her quiet mannerisms, air of reflection, and diligent work ethic had infused the entire structure and staff with a sense of purpose and confidence in the future direction.

Which was why he was here on this particular Wednesday morning. Summer was now in full bloom. Everywhere within the building were flowers of all kinds, grown on the grounds and cultivated by a paid gardener, along with numerous volunteering seniors, whose well-acquired cultivation skills surrounded the hospice with wonderful palettes of colour.

Scarlett turned around and expressed her surprise at the other presence in the room.

"How long have you been standing there?" she asked.

"Long enough to see that it's not up to you to do the clean-up when we have others for that task. You're the director, and you should be directing," the vicar replied.

"It's called therapy," she countered with what could only be a tired smile. "This room has the smell of love in it," Scarlett said, almost in a whisper. She made a show of pretending to smell the air around her. "I have seen so many conversations that I wasn't privy to take place in this room. But through the glass I could still see that they were beautiful and meaningful. This is the staging area of this building, Tom. It's conversations that have taken place here that prepared so many for the next stage of their journey."

The vicar watched as she ran her hands over the books and pamphlets, as if caressing a lover. She straightened a painting depicting a sunset (or was it a sunrise, he wondered) and eventually turned to face him directly.

He smiled. "Words like you just uttered here have given this sacred place its own scriptures, its own meaning. You have a way with expressing thoughts that seem to emerge from the future, not the past, and they come with a sense of hope. I can't tell you how many times I have expressed my thanks to God that you said yes to coming here. You have turned this place into a sanctuary of preparation, and not just pain."

They were quiet following this, and before she turned to resume her work he asked, "What say I take you out for some dinner? I know the day's been long for you."

He was delighted when she nodded thankfully, and twenty minutes later they had a table by the window of the White Horse restaurant, sharing wine and splitting a Margherita pizza. Early enough that the drinking crowd hadn't yet arrived, they relished the comfortable quiet.

"So, to what do I owe this delightful pleasure?" Scarlett asked.

Spelling wiped the corner of his mouth, placed both hands on the table, and replied, "You likely know that we had a meeting with some of the board last week, doing our usual routine of examining the budget for the fall." When she didn't respond, he went on. "It goes without exaggeration, Scarlett, that the response to your leadership at St. Anne's has been universally positive and affirming. But we all felt you have paid a price for all your efforts and sacrifice. You're looking overly tired and we're a bit worried. I know you'll deny it, but ..."

"No, they're right," she interjected, surprising him. Scarlett put her fork down, placed her hands in her lap, and leaned forward. "I so much wanted to make the hospice the place it could be that I think I went with too little sleep, too little time for myself. But don't think it a sacrifice, Tom. I loved every second of it. The board has given me an opportunity that few could even dream of, and

I've wanted to return the favour by turning St. Anne's into a haven for the spirit and the body."

With a natural habit, the vicar lifted his glass towards that of his companion and said, "To a beautiful partnership, then. Thank you for understanding, Scarlett. I was expecting something of a battle, but, as I am discovering in delightful fashion, you have once again surprised me."

She joined her glass to his before asking, "What is the board asking of me?"

"Well, they're pretty firm on the idea of you taking a couple of weeks to yourself and recharging your batteries. Delores totally agrees and says she'll be fine covering for you during that time." He sighed. "It's summer, Scarlett – summer in England and Europe - and its glorious. Just do what you need to do."

And just what do I need to do? she thought to herself later. She could return to Canada to visit relatives; in fact, she probably should at some point. Yet she knew that would hardly constitute a rest. Being on the edge of the English Channel, the pleasure of France, the ruggedness of Germany or Austria, or the sunny delights of Portugal or Spain always beckoned and were only a few hours away.

Scarlett dozed off in the hot bath, her wine glass now emptied. The day had been long, but the thought of relaxing for a couple of weeks brought a comforting leisure in that fatigue.

Waking up with a start a few minutes later, Scarlett towelled off and pulled on her robe. In her mind, she was already settled on her vacation destination, and she sat at her computer and began researching.

6

Scarlett was surprised to note that the gorgeous sun had brought out some freckles on her arm as she rested it on the driver's window. She had rented the small yellow Fiat in Messina, Sicily, after taking the ferry over from the famous "toe" of the Italian mainland. Everything she took in was beautiful, especially the Mediterranean, as it took everything the sun lavished upon it and thrust it back onto the surrounding hillsides.

She was bound for Taormina, further down the east coast of the island and nestled high up the hills overlooking the sea. Traffic was brisk, as it was the summer tourist season, but she was thankful to be back driving on the right side of the highway after the months of adjusting to the contrary British practice.

The road up to Taormina was as steep as anything she had driven in her life – precarious, hairpin turns, and little in the way of guard rails to prevent a vehicle from careening over the cliff. Yet it was invigorating, as that adventurous part of her rose in response. Scarlett frequently had to pull to the side of the narrow road to make room for oncoming vehicles, leaving her riding the clutch to gain momentum for moving ever upward once more.

Taormina perched precariously on the side of the cliff and seemed to threaten to fall away at any moment. But it was beautiful – one of the most idyllic locations she had ever witnessed, though she could only capture fleeting glimpses to keep from driving off into the abyss.

But her destination was at the very top of the hill – a tiny community called Castelmola, and the uniquely situated Hotel Villa Sonia.

Scarlett finally relaxed her pent-up nerves as she pulled into an impossibly narrow parking spot on an impossibly narrow strip of road. She was greeted by a front foyer full of spartan colours with an open entranceway to a furnished terrace just beyond. She confirmed her reservation, confirmed her credit card information, and then proceeded up the narrow stairs to her floor.

Her room, perfectly proportioned, and with a quaint mixture of old and modern furniture, had a vast view of the Ionian Sea as it spread to every horizon. The sun was brilliant, and under that illuminating celestial canopy everything seemed alive and yet tranquil. She permitted her gaze to scan the north and east, along the roadway she had just travelled from Messina. Shifting her gaze along the shore to the south, she spotted the road continuing on its journey to Catania near the bottom of the island. Everything was full of rustic browns and greens, with the brilliant aquamarine blue of the water never far from view.

Scarlett thought she might rest, but planned to do so outside, by the pool, and in the warmth of the sun. She unpacked her one suitcase and shifted from her slacks and short-sleeved blouse into a one-piece burnt orange swim-suit. Grabbing her sunglasses and lotion, she proceeded out the rear of the building and was confronted by two compelling sights.

The first was the pool itself, shimmering, and wending its way along a curved path lined with limestone columns. Candles floated in the water. Two restaurants bordered the pool, populated by a number of sunseekers seated at the tables, enjoying the Mediterranean fare.

The other view was as vast as the sky itself. The land-scape, largely level and mostly sparse, rose from north and south to form the peak of Mt. Etna – the island's iconic volcano that occasionally sprang to life with various erup-tions every few years. Even now, she could spot circling plumes of both steam and smoke moving around its highest regions. There were no rumblings, but its presence reminded everyone around it that things could change in an instant. She gave it no further thought, and found a lounge chair to her liking near a quiet spot at the rear of the pool.

Scarlett laid out her large hotel towel, grabbed her *Fodors* travel book on Sicily, and settled in for a sunny read.

Her intentions didn't last long; within minutes she nodded off under the warm embrace of the sun.

Clearly, the drive had exhausted her, for as she emerged from her slumber it was near to dinner time. Noticing the goosebumps on her arms, she surmised that the late-after-noon chill in the air had awoken her. The pool area, largely abandoned, was quiet. But the restaurant personnel were keeping busy, setting dining tables and preparing a smörgåsbord table, complete with flowers and candles, in preparation for the evening meal.

She leisurely showered, and took her time with her hair. This wasn't for anyone but herself – it had been months since she had been able to pamper herself for an evening out. She put on a long floral dress and covered her arms and shoulders with a royal navy blue stole and her feet with low leather heels. To this ensemble she added drop earrings and a tiny purse.

She arrived just before any evening rush, and was escorted to a table situated between two walls. One of these was a frescoed expanse on which hung some ornate wooden carvings and an ancient cart wheel. It added to a sense of permanence, she realized. The other was highlighted by a series of arches, each lined by fire-baked bricks. Through each opening was a beautifully situated panorama of Etna.

She ordered some local red wine and, accepting the waiter's suggestion, ordered Pesto alla trapanese, a local dish consisting of noodles in a rich basil pesto sauce. Then she opened up *Fodors* travel book on Sicily and began reading in earnest.

Scarlett had never considered a vacation to this region, but being away from Canada for all these months had caused her to think of her family more often – especially Nan, her grandmother, who had passed away years earlier but whom she was extremely close to. She had never known her grandfather, since he was killed on this island during the Second World War during the Canadian invasion of the southern shore. Nan had informed Scarlett that her husband had been buried after his death, and that has his body had been moved a few years later to a special Canadian Commonwealth cemetery along with hundreds of others.

"I was never able to visit your grandfather's grave," she

informed Scarlett a year before her passing. "Maybe someday you can go there for me, dear, and lay some flowers on his grave. He would like that."

When Tom had offered her a couple of weeks off, Scarlett decided to carry out that wish. She brought only two books with her on the trip – Fodors, and *The Italian Campaign: The 1st Canadian Infantry Division and the Invasion of Sicily*. She hadn't yet dug into the latter, but the former had provided treasures of information and background. She had already discovered some basic things, such as Sicily being the largest island in the Mediterranean, and Etna being the tallest active volcano in Europe. The vast island maintained a rich and unique culture, especially in areas like the arts, music, literature, architecture, and, naturally, cuisine.

By the time she had finished perusing the various invasions of the island throughout history – modern and ancient – her dinner had arrived. Two men, dressed in local custom, came near her table. One expertly worked a violin, while the other moved the bellows of an accordion and sang famous Sicilian songs in a warm and inviting voice. Scarlett's face flushed as other patrons looked in her direction and smiled. They were actually very good entertainers, and she was certain, given that she was a single woman at a table, that they were performing love songs for her benefit.

Eventually they moved on to other tables, leaving her to lazily finish her meal with the assistance of a follow-up glass of wine. She could feel its warming effects despite the chill in the air.

The atmosphere was filled with sounds of music, laughter, and the occasional splash of someone frolicking in the moonlit pool. Off in the distance was the eerie silhouette of the great Etna – its details hidden in the dark, but its outline domineering. She had already made a mental note to check into the possibility of any tours to the peak, and wondered just how dangerous that might be.

She later finished a coffee, along with a flourless orange cake with caramel sauce for dessert, before heading back to her room. Scarlett had thought of walking along the perimeter of the hotel at the peak but, feeling the effects of the wine, opted to get some sleep before getting a good start in the morning. She realized, as she closed her eyes for the night, that she hadn't once thought of St. Anne's or Mulladore. She smiled to herself, thinking that Vicar Tom would be pleased with that bit of news.

Scarlett was surprised to wake early, feeling no ill-effects from the wine and the previous day's travel. After breakfasting, she drove down the steep hills to the shore, ahead of the morning traffic. News alerts had spoken of unusual activity at Etna's peak, resulting in a cancellation of all tours or visitors for the next few days. Disappointed, it did provide her opportunity to explore other delights on this island.

She adjusted her schedule, downsizing it to a more relaxed day. Exploring Taormina was always highly appealing because of its exquisite postcard-like qualities and the welcoming look of its beaches. And for the evening, she booked herself a reservation, prior to leaving England, for the first of three amphitheatre shows performed acoustically by a British pop star.

Instead of touring the various beaches in the region, Scarlett, fully intrigued by the pebbled Isola Bella waterfront, settled in with a beach chair, some bottled water, and the hefty *The Italian Campaign: The 1st Canadian Infantry*

Division and the Invasion of Sicily. Occasionally she took a break from reading and fell in love with the view of Taormina from the water itself. She swam out to the tiny lushly vegetated islet jutting out into the water, and then walked back along the narrow strip of beach linking it to the mainland.

She performed the same routine late in the morning, then settled in for more reading. If the sight of a female tourist reading a thick volume on World War Two history struck anyone as odd, she never noticed.

Scarlett slowly opened her eyes when the sound of a small ferry cruised along parallel to the waterfront, its occupants shrieking with delight. The book was on her lap and her toes were in the pebbles. It was only as she fetched her watch from her bag that she realized she had slept for two hours, and that it was already mid-afternoon. She slowly rose, packed her belongings, and proceeded in the car back up to the Villa Sonia, finding the harrowing drive somewhat easier with the practice.

She retrieved her key from the front desk, along with one of the shiny green apples in a bowl on the counter, and walked to her room. Still feeling drowsy from all those hours in the sun and water, she permitted her body to be caressed by the fresh linen sheets of the bed and fell directly back to sleep.

Instead of going to dinner, Scarlett took a long soak in a hot bath and kept reading about how Canadian troops experienced great difficulty landing in the heavy surf of Sicily – a number drowned, weighted down by the forty pounds of gear each bore on their backs. This was all in preparation for her journey tomorrow, in hopes she would locate her grandfather's grave and fulfill an old promise.

Three hours later, as the sun set over the back of the hills, leaving the town in the beginnings of a sultry darkness, she was seated halfway up the semi-circular outdoor theatre on a stone seat. Despite the slight discomfort, the effect was one of being transported into the ancient past.

Teatro Antico was one of the most famous theatres around the Mediterranean. From its seats, one could see the coast stretching off to the south and Etna in the distance. It had been constructed three centuries before Christ by the Greeks but had been modified later by the Romans by the addition of columns and statues. It vaunted porticos and even a sunken place for an orchestra, but the centre of it all was the small intimate stage, situated between the audience and the vast expanse of the sea.

Scarlett had purchased a glass of the sweet locally grown Malvasia wine. As she waited for the concert to commence, she perused the thin program provided at her entrance. Scarlett looked around to see that every seat was occupied, and that the lights of the town around the theatre had been dimmed in honour of the concert.

For the next ninety minutes she permitted her spirit to sway along with the tones of the British baritone performer, who had begun his own career at the time of the Beatles and now offered a vast array of hits he had created over the decades since. His hair was cropped and grey, his body trim and toned, and his tanned features and pleasant voice made for an intimate occasion. She sang along with others as some of the more famous hits were performed, and placed the program in her small purse as a momentum of a warm and entertaining evening.

Scarlett filed out with the others and began the short but steep climb up the steps to her hotel. Her legs were burning with exertion as she arrived back in her room. Unlike the previous evening, the air was now hot, almost sticky, and just a bit stifling. She thought of turning on the air conditioning but instead slid open the portico door, permitting the breeze to work its way through the room. She took off her dress and earrings, along with the pearl necklace that had been her mothers, and climbed into bed in only her undergarments.

And there, under the watching eye of the great volcano, she fell asleep with the thoughts of war and love, death and life, history and the present, running through her mind.

7

Scarlett checked the map while munching on a bagel she had grabbed from the breakfast bar at the Villa Sonia. By hugging the coast road along the Ionian Sea, the trip was supposed to be only an hour from Taormina to Catania, an ancient sea port town on the island east coast with a population of roughly 300,000 inhabitants. It was the main staging location for visits to Mt. Etna, being situated near its base.

But that wasn't where she was headed. Today, her destination was the ultimate purpose for this welcome vacation: the Catania War Cemetery. It served as one of the three Commonwealth cemeteries on the island that held the final remains of Canadian soldiers killed in the summer invasion of 1943 during World War Two.

Scarlett had done as much research as she could prior to leaving England, and had discovered her grandfather's name in a database listing those Canadians honoured in the cemetery. Corporal Jeffrey Carlyle had successfully landed on the sandy beach as one of the frontline troops of the

Canadian First Division, only to be cut down the next week by a German sniper hiding in some brush – one of 500 killed over the next five weeks. Called Operation Husky, the invasion, as part of a broader Allied effort, was a success, and the forces then moved on to invade Italy, having driven the Germans and Italians off the island.

For those left behind, rough graves had been dug, seemingly forgotten in the Sicilian volcanic earth, as the world's attention moved northward, to Italy, D-Day, and finally the defeat of the German forces. Scarlett had read of how opposition mounted the further the Canadians pushed into Sicily. Sadly, her grandfather had paid the ultimate price.

"I think he honestly thought he was going to be okay," Nan had told Scarlett when she was a young child. They had been married only the year before, in the thick of the conflict, knowing that he would inevitably be shipped overseas. When Jeffrey Carlyle had boarded the troopship in Halifax, his wife was already pregnant with the child that would eventually become Scarlett's mother. He never returned, leaving a daughter without a father, a wife without her new husband, and a granddaughter who would never had the privilege of knowing him.

Thinking on it now on the roadway to Catania, she wondered how it was that Nan had never remarried. Seriously, she had chosen to live alone for the remaining seventy years, until her death. *Who does that anymore?* she asked herself out loud. Today, loads of couples never get married, and they frequently split up as often as they hook up. Life was often a series of romantic relationships, one after another, and sometimes the ultimate bliss never arrived.

Nan had lived in a different time, and Scarlett understood the strengths and weaknesses of what was called the Greatest Generation. Nevertheless, the love story between Jeffrey and Nan lingered in her mind in almost legendary fashion – a love that endured even when ended by war.

She looked up in time to see the turnoff from the A-19 to the Commonwealth War Cemetery and felt an inner sense of expectation, mixed with sadness. As she pulled up to the front entrance, Scarlett discovered that no vehicles were permitted within the cemetery itself, so she parked her vehicle along the side of the road. The place seemed abandoned, with no other vehicles or people present.

She emerged from the driver's seat, with her sunhat, darkened polaroid glasses, and a cellphone in hand for photos. A sign by the front gate said that visitors were welcome anytime and that the location never closed. She passed through the gate and walked the 500 metres to the official entrance. There she discovered plaques describing the cemetery, along with books, placed within a small shelter, that listed the names of the dead and their location among the rows of white stone slabs, which spread off uniformly in all directions. Lifting her eyes above the scene, she could see the impressive slopes of Etna sweeping down towards the graves as if in deference to their sacrifice.

Scarlett quickly scanned her *Fodors* and learned that 2,135 Commonwealth soldiers were buried in the site – 113 of them unidentified. She could see steps leading up to a thin obelisk. On its top was a small cross, made of the same material as the gravestones.

Being the only person in sight, she began meandering along the central pathway before mounting the stairs to the obelisk. Her spirit grew slightly troubled at the condition of the stairs. They were crumbling in parts, badly stained in others, and they provided an overall aura of lack of proper care. A plaque at the base of the spire commemorated the dead and elaborated on the British Commonwealth and its responsibility for its various war cemeteries around the world.

The map at the front gate had given the locations of the various sections of the site where nationalities were recognized, and she worked her way towards the Canadian area. It was symmetrical, like the others, with a small strip of pebbles and dirt running along in front of the grave stones. The names engraved on the off-white surfaces weren't in alphabetical order. Instead, they were in the order in which the soldiers had fallen. That caused Scarlett to walk to the beginning of the display, knowing that her grandfather had fallen in the first week of the invasion.

Her eyes scanned the engravings even as they misted. Someone had placed small Canadian flags beside each stone and they were beautiful in their multitude. The passing by of each stone only meant that her quest was ever nearer.

And then, at last, it was there – four stones from the end, and content in its companionship. Before reading anything, she reached out and allowed her fingers to caress its outline – straight on its sides, slightly curved on the top. Then her gaze lowered and fell into the mystery of the words.

MASTER CORPORAL
JEFFREY ALBERT CARLYLE
CANADIAN FIRST DIVISION
July 1943 – Age 27

A maple leaf engraved in a circle lingered above the inscription, while a tall thin cross nestled below it. Scarlett knelt as her forefinger traced each letter before her. Decades fell away as she embraced the man she never knew. Without him she wouldn't be here, she knew. But that was true twice over. His death, like millions of others, had provided her the honour of living. She felt overcome with debt.

She had seen, copied, and kept the few pictures there were of the man. Lean, like everyone else of his generation, he appeared tall, with medium length hair and a wistful smile. The black and white photos gave no indication of his eye colour or whether his skin was tanned. One image showed him leaning over the oars of a rowboat, grinning at the photographer. Another had him walking along with his mother through a downtown Halifax street. Her favourite image was of him sitting on some kind of bench overlooking the ocean, a pipe in his hand and khaki cap on his head. It was obviously summer, but the far away reflective look in his gaze somehow drew her to him over the years.

Scarlett stood with her hand resting on the stone and grew quiescent. Tears were on her face but she didn't really notice. Her mind took in the breadth of what she saw here – death everywhere. Her heart lifted in recognition, for death was something – a visitor, a dread, a surety, a *reality* – and she had learned not to turn her eyes or emotions away from it. Her professional work had inculcated this durability within her, but, as she realized now, so had this relationship with a grandfather she had never known.

Yet she understood him better than she might have realized in past years, simply because Nan had told her, answering every query of her granddaughter and, in the process, fleshing out what had once been only a mystic presence that had suspended itself over the family.

And now, here she was: face to face with history and a reality. He had walked this land, likely laughed and faced fear on it, and had ultimately breathed his last somewhere near here. Her grandmother had recounted the final words he gave her before heading off to war: "Nothing endures that isn't fought for." That insight now made sense to her. Fighting, for him, wasn't about responding in the moment, but protecting that in humanity which was most dear by giving one's own life for it, if one had to.

Which was what Jeffrey Carlyle had done, here in this beautiful but faraway place. He had sanctified the future by sacrificing his own future.

It takes someone used to death to not be so intimidated by it, Scarlett realized. And that included her. In this place, at this time, death was something that might be respected. It wasn't so much a friend as it was an ally – capable, when required, of doing something meritorious, despite its harsh and permanent demeanour.

Again, her heart lifted in understanding and recognition – and acknowledgement. She reached into her pocket and brought out a brooch that once belonged to her grandmother, having been presented to her by Jeffrey on the day of their engagement. It was a golden maple leaf, much like the one on the gravestone, but with a navy-blue background. Scarlett had treasured it for years, but knew that it had now found its rightful resting place.

It was only as she patted down the grass to lay the piece at the stone's base that she noted a further inscription she had missed earlier. The sight of it filled her with tears in an instant, for she already possessed a heart that understood its message:

ALL IS NOT FINISHED

Scarlett laid the brooch directly beneath the letters and stood to leave, wiping away tears that were now flowing easily and welcomely down her cheeks. She had come to this place to fulfill a promise to her grandmother and realized she had just received a promise in return.

8

"It went well, then?"

Scarlett heard the voice from a distance as she unloaded groceries from the car following her return from Sicily. She had come home to an empty fridge and a vacant wine rack, and had just bought ample supplies for both at the supermarket in Whitfield. She turned to spot the voice's source and saw Bert Wynman's countenance smiling at her over his stone fence.

"Just back," she responded, before holding up the bag containing some wine, and adding, "and I'm ready for a neighbourly visit."

He came by a half-hour later, with a large wedge of Tunworth cheese that he had bought at the same Whitfield market earlier in the day. The heat of the afternoon sun was still too strong, so they chose to sit in patio chairs, outside and under the protective shade of a cedar trellis, now partially overgrown by vines.

Scarlett filled the next hour recounting the beauty of Taormina, the hairpin turns, and, finally, her emotional journey to the Catania cemetery. He noted, from her misty eyes, that the memory of her grandfather still lingered.

"I had an uncle that served there – in Sicily, I mean. He was part of British General Montgomery's forces, but made it back after the Italian campaign ended. He lived not far from Dover actually, but he never spoke of the horrors they endured there. Just like the rest of his war chums."

She thought about this for a moment, then said, "My grandfather never got that opportunity – to return to Canada with his pals. I always found that kind of sad. You spend three years of your life defending your country, only to get killed in action and buried somewhere else."

Unsure how to respond, her guest opted to take the conversation in a different direction.

"Do you feel rested and ready for St. Anne's?"

Scarlett looked up and smiled, leading him to believe that she knew exactly what he was doing. "I feel somewhat rested, I suppose," she offered, "but I think I'm better prepared for the hospice."

"How so?" he pressed.

She sighed before imbibing a bit more wine. "I've been thinking about that. Dealing with death as I have done over these last years, between Canada and here, you get to see it as one case at a time. The first passing under your watch is traumatic, as is the next, and the next. But at some point, you realize that the emotions aren't as erratic and you settle in to this relationship with death – the same death that everyone else so greatly fears. You're never comfortable with it, but it doesn't terrorize you or take up your personal resources and stamina as much as it once did. And just like that, you find it has moved into the hospice, almost as a guest."

Scarlett looked up to see Bert regarding her with mild surprise.

"What?" she asked.

"Are your observation skills that attuned?" he began. "You just shared some profound thoughts that go a long way to explaining why you are as strong as you are."

"You'd better explain that, Bert."

He went on blithely, as if he hadn't heard her. "I know that a hospice is meant to take the sting out of the end of life experience. It draws in families, friends, and even staff I suppose, into one of the most exquisite of human dramas. But you have taken it a step further, haven't you? You've depersonalized it. It's now a facet of life, not merely a Rite of Passage. For you, it is ever-present, like life itself, and you endure its devastating actions because you've kept its company most of your adult life."

The wine had not yet reached Scarlett's brain, but it was beginning to affect her senses. What her neighbour had just observed was full of profundity. There wasn't anything that Bert had uttered that wasn't, in fact, true, and that hadn't been proved true in her life. The thing was: she had never really understood that until now.

She wanted to explore his thoughts further when he, instead, asked, "You implied that the atmosphere of the cemetery in Sicily had a different kind of effect on you. How do you mean?"

In response to his question, Scarlett shifted gears easily enough, though she regretted moving on from the observation he had made just a minute ago.

"Well, if working with end-of-life communities permits death to slowly affect you over time, one instance following another, Sicily was the exact opposite."

"Meaning?"

"Meaning death at that level is more like being swallowed up in history – not gradually, but as a baptism of sudden tragedy and realization. It's the only show in town, the centre of all attention. And it's the entity left standing at the end the day, when all else has fallen away. But once you're through that, death starts to become more personalized. That's what happened to me in Sicily. Things went from death on a grand scale to an individual story of a man who gave his life for his country."

They were both quiet for a time before Bert leaned forward to top up their glasses and carve her a piece of cheese. Neither was sure where to take the conversation next. He broke the silence.

"I actually think those are beautiful thoughts, Scarlett. That idea of the hospice taking death from small to large, while the cemetery in Sicily went the opposite direction, is remarkable. I suppose the sad part is that at the end of the day, death wins – it's over.

She glanced up, eyes flaring, as if angry, leaving him to wonder what he had done to prompt such a response. She leaned forward on the sofa, looking at her hands.

"Funny you should say that," Scarlett said. "I was laying something at the base of the gravestone, a memento, and I discovered a further piece of writing hidden behind the grass. Know what it said?"

He shrugged, unsure where she was headed with this.

"Only four words – *All Is Not Finished.* And I believe that's true. Death doesn't get the last word. It doesn't get to take the final bow because the play, with all the drama, isn't over. There's another act."

"What act?" he said sharply. "Come now, Scarlett, don't

delude yourself. You've done fine to this point, remarkably so, actually. You've encountered death in numerous adventures, personal and grand, and you have come to terms with it. But that's because of the finality of it. All is death in the end. Those who know it live life to the full."

Quietness again. Then, to his surprise, she turned to him and asked the question that robbed him of his sleep for the rest of the night: "Is that what you have, then, Bert – life to the full?"

He was taken aback at her boldness – a boldness that, to his mind, bordered on insolence. And, to his surprise, he was at a loss for a response. He didn't know how to take her and, worse still, he didn't really have an answer to her query.

"Well, that's certainly what I'm attempting to do, and I think I've done rather well at it." He looked at her directly after he said this, but couldn't hold his gaze to hers. For the first time in their brief relationship there seemed to be some kind of distance – an expanse which he couldn't cross.

Scarlett knew she had gone too far and sought to walk it back. "I'm sorry, Bert. I didn't mean that in any pejorative way. It's just that moments where I've observed death not gaining the upper hand were when friends and loved ones gave those final days a sense of the triumphant. And by your own admission, you endeavour to keep any close attachment at a distance. It saves entanglements, I suspect, but I have wondered at times if it isn't lonely."

She could tell he was considering leaving, but then Bert sat back and sighed. "It's not as though I haven't been around, you know," he said, finally, and a tad defensively. "I have lost relatives over the years, though my parents died when I was young. And as far as friends go, well, there have been many, but of the professional kind."

His host was about to interject, but then sensed he wasn't finished.

"But you're right, I suppose – living alone is by choice, and I don't regret it. It doesn't keep me from respecting the work you do and the insights you have, like the ones you spoke of earlier."

She sensed he had more to add, but then he abruptly stood. "I should probably get back, since it's late." His words were brusque, despite his attempted attitude of nonchalance. Scarlett quickly rushed into the kitchen to wrap the Tunworth cheese for him to cart home, but he was already out the door after mumbling something about being glad she had a good vacation.

His shadowed form moved down the path to the road, from where she could no longer spot him. Eventually, the interior lights of his home came on, and she saw him fumbling in the kitchen.

Could I have been any more impulsive? she asked herself. Excuses paraded in front of her mind – travel fatigue, the wine, his hyper-sensitivity and misunderstanding – but these were just deflections. Unlike a good neighbour, Scarlett had pushed too far and he had, in response, put himself at an emotional distance.

The sleep, so yearned for now that she was home, never came, and sometime during the tossing and turning, Scarlett understood she had work to do to restore a familial relationship that was still in its early stages. *All is not finished,* she thought – fitting.

9

***

Bert Wynman still smarted from what he could only conclude was his neighbour's unwarranted criticism. He hadn't slept at all on the night of their discussion. After tossing for two hours on his mattress, he chose to take an arduous walk along the country lanes leading from his residence towards the coastline, miles in the distance. Even as his legs protested the pace, he found that anger still dominated his emotions.

Taking a moment to wait for traffic to pass at a roundabout, he caught the welcome scent of the ocean air blowing up and over the white limestone cliffs. He continued until he arrived at the crest of the highest promontory overlooking Dover itself. His eyes traced the two piers stretching out into the channel like two lengthy arms until they finally closed in on one another, as if in embrace, providing protection to the harbour and just enough of an opening to permit the fishing boats and pleasure craft out into the deeper water.

Off in the southern horizon, he caught the glow of the French port of Calais reflected in the wispy clouds nestled close over the water. His gaze drew closer, once again, onto the port town below. Dover had never become anything other than a picturesque testimony to the beauty of the south of England. The long piers for the ferries to France and Belgium protected the small gathering of some fifty sailboats tied up for the night.

Bert sat on a bench near the cliff's edge, the gentle breeze off the water refreshing his face. He cast his gaze about at nothing in particular. His spirit had quieted down as he considered just how fond he had become of Scarlett – not in any romantic sense that he could tell, but because of her open countenance and her willingness to gently probe past his natural reserve to establish some kind of connection.

And that had turned out to be the problem – she had pushed too far, surprisingly. He had mentioned to her enough times that his privacy was important to him, and, up until now, she had permitted her neighbour his requested emotional distance. He presumed she had learned that skill as part and parcel of the lessons of her profession. Don't get too attached. Allow people their space for the journey. Keep the pain at a distance so as not to be overly susceptible to the waves of a grief that would relentlessly crash on her shore.

Why, then, her persistence hours earlier? Bert recalled the context of that conversation – her holiday visit to Sicily, and the military graveyard experience – and graciously conceded the seriousness of her journey through history, and how that might have placed her in a different state of mind.

He didn't know why, or even how, but his Canadian friend had somehow penetrated his carefully practiced reserve with little effort. And she had accomplished it before he had even noticed. He smiled, watching a cabin cruiser pleasure vessel slip in through the entrance to the harbour at this late hour, its running lights illuminating the water around it and its inboard offering a quiet throb. He realized how similar its arrival was to Scarlett's presence in his life.

He was old enough, and practiced enough, to learn the skills of developing friendships or working relationships with women of various ages without allowing them to follow the familiar paths of physical attraction – unless it was what they both desired, of course. But Scarlett's presence had come into his life at a level he wasn't prepared for. She was a friend, yes, even if only in the beginning stages. Yet he had to admit to himself that all his previous relational experiences hadn't prepared him for this woman's effect on his intellectual sentiments. That gentle intrusion, welcome and surprising as it was, prompted a new possibility in his understanding: had she, unknowingly, uncovered a part of him he never knew existed?

His mind began running down that corridor of thought, as if chasing some elusive presence into a dimension he hadn't visited previously. Bert had to confess that he had carefully crafted his life so as to limit such temptations, that he had perhaps failed to explore the depths of his own soul more insightfully.

Bert sighed. He lifted his gaze out over the channel that had so become an inspiration and mooring point for his life – the entirety of it – and felt what he could only term a "summoning." Despite his age and practiced pattern of limiting risks, he understood that he was chasing the beguiling spirit of Scarlett into unknown territory. And what surprised him more was that he wasn't alarmed by that new bit of knowledge.

He looked out again to the channel's expanse and the opaque lights of Calais. The omnipresent sense of distance acted upon him, and his spirit was strangely calmed, serene even. Somehow, he understood that what he once knew of himself was not what he was now. He acknowledged that he wasn't necessarily deeper with that awareness, but he was broader, more expansive. And that change could be credited only to his new neighbour over the wall.

Bert Wynman gave a quiet *adieu* to the eternal water and the glorious white cliffs that had so grounded his life and then began working his way home, sensing the gentle seismic shift that had just occurred within him.

At the same time, Scarlett regretted never having the chance to smooth things over with Bert, since that same week when the world seemed to have turned upside down.

At the end of her vacation, while waiting for her flight, she had spotted a number of fellow passengers gathered beneath a television screen which was airing an urgent BBC report about a virus centred in China that was now in the process of spreading across the globe. Across the bottom of the display appeared the word destined to preoccupy every country in the world: CORONAVIRUS.

By the time she returned to the hospice, on the day following her awkward exchange with Bert, news reports were affirming that seniors were most at risk in what was about to become a global pandemic. Though British health authorities had maintained that Britain's risk was "very low," alerts started coming in from both York and Brighton that Chinese nationals studying in those locations had introduced what was termed Covid-19 to the country.

At the staff meeting on that first morning of her return, an executive team from the country's National Health Service (NHS) provided a briefing on the impending danger. What they intimated was far different than what was being released to the public. Since the nation's travel and immigration policies were some of the most liberal in the world, the health officials warned of the possibility of a rapid expansion of the virus, especially among the elderly, in the coming weeks. Whitfield and the south of England were especially vulnerable due to the size of the elderly population and the number of institutions dedicated to their care.

When Scarlett inquired of them what precautions St. Andrew's might embark on, she was met with a blank look in return.

"These are early days," the man said. "Though we've known of this virus for some time, it was our hope that it wouldn't reach these shores."

"But it has," Scarlett interjected. "Is there nothing we can do – in preparation, I mean?"

He looked at her sympathetically. "Of course, there are always precautions. And we do have protocols in place for just such an occasion. I'll get my staff to email all the seniors' facilities in this region, starting with St. Anne's. Clearly, a heightened hygiene protocol would be wise. And since the virus plays havoc with the respiratory system, it would be wise to stock up on masks and ventilators. We'll help with those, if we can."

He threw up his hands in frustration. "I'm sorry we can't help more, Ms. Carlyle. We're just not sure what we're dealing with at this precise moment. I'm afraid we'll have to learn and adapt the further we get into this, and then I'll be able to tell you more."

After he left, Delores Pampau, who had been in charge during Scarlett's absence, placed the facility on skeleton staff, and joined the remainder of the workers in the staff lunch room to ponder what had just been said.

"Okay, I'm the first to say that I'm in unfamiliar territory here," Scarlett began. "Back in Canada, a number of years ago, we had the SARS pandemic. It was the first of the 21st century for us. From the outset, it was clear that we weren't really prepared for it. It threatened to undermine our entire health system, but we caught a break. The virus turned out to be weak, and couldn't last out there in society for any real length of time. When it was over there was a lot of hand-wringing, passing of the buck, and the realization that we got lucky. But that entire episode taught us that we could have done better; we could have been more prepared."

Everyone was watching her keenly, concern impressed on each face. She thought of how they each looked cautious, and perhaps frightened, about the unknown.

"Let's not bother waiting around for the HIS to send us their files," she continued. And for the next fifteen minutes Scarlett assigned duties to some of the staff, including research on the origins of the virus in China, the best practices learned in places like Africa and Thailand about proper quarantine methods in recent outbreaks in those regions, and, perhaps most importantly, what would be the proper protocols if anyone at St. Anne's contracted the virus.

The mood at St. Anne's became decidedly sombre, as if they were preparing for some kind of invasion, without knowing at what time it would strike. Scarlett was impressed with her staff and their sense of purpose, especially as it regarded their patients. Those staying at St. Anne's could lodge there for their final three months of life, so there was a determined effort to keep the approaching storm away from them and their families.

But it remained a difficult thing to keep the oncoming threat at arm's length when the BBC reported, on an hourly basis, the rise in cases in the succeeding days. Within the first week, the number of cases in the country had gone from two to just over two thousand, and it was clear there would be no stopping the increase. Since the first cases were discovered only a few miles away in Kent, and then in Brighton, nearby on the southern coast, everyone understood that Whitfield would be in the immediate path of the calamity. Slowly, almost defiantly, the virus began striking individuals and families in Royal Tunbridge Wells, Sittingbourne, Maidstone, and, inevitably, Dover.

Scarlett, along with Delores and a few others, opted to remain day and night at the hospice to oversee the round-the-clock efforts in preparation for the virus. A number of times each day her thoughts wandered to Bert Wynman and the need for her attention towards restoring the neighbourliness they had previously enjoyed. His presence wasn't apparent whenever she returned home to attend to a few maintenance items, although she thought she spotted him driving away early one evening. Once again, she admonished herself for her impudence, especially now that she had to dedicate her constant efforts to St. Anne's.

Then, one Thursday afternoon, before she could do anything about Bert, word came from Delores that one of their kitchen staff had become sick, gone to be tested, and telephoned to confirm that she was Whitfield's first authenticated case of COVID-19. The invasion had arrived.

10

Troubling weeks turned into a devastating two months, as COVID ravaged its way through Kent, Britain, and most of the world. The BBC was sorry to report that 41,405 citizens had died by the second month anniversary of the first case. Britain had the world's fourth-highest death rate per capita among major countries. Most troubling of all for Scarlett and her staff was the announcement that more than 90% of those dying had underlying illnesses or were over 60 years of age. The infection rate was higher in seniors' homes and hospices than in any other sector.

The infection only tarried in southern England for a few days before it transitioned its way to the northern part of the country and into Ireland. The UK government had just imposed a stay-at-home order. All non-essential travel had been banned. All schools, businesses, public facilities, and place of worship were closed down completely, including the church of St. Anne's. Thousands chafed when it was announced that the police were empowered to enforce all of these measures. Then Parliament enacted the Coronavirus Act 2020, which gave the police more oversight and emergency powers for the government – a measure that hadn't been used since World War Two.

The National Health Service worked around the clock in Wales, England, Ireland, and Scotland to raise hospital capacity, setting up temporary critical care hospitals, including in facilities like St. Anne's Hospice, where those in their dying days and weeks were especially vulnerable to a virus no one had heard of a mere six month ago.

From the moment that Claire, the assistant cook in the kitchen, informed hospice administrators that the local hospital had confirmed she had COVID, Scarlett knew she was entering a whole new world of public health dilemma, and that she would be expected to take the lead in any kind of response. Fortunately, the Canadian SARS experience had helped her to see what happened when public fear outdistanced the ability of health authorities to provide assurance, and the reverse that occurred when the virus ran out of steam. Scarlett knew instinctively that her life would resemble more of a rollercoaster ride than the steady routine of a seasoned hospital administrator.

She spent numerous nights at the hospice, despite the protestations of Reverend Spelling that she remove herself from any danger by retreating to Mulladore in confines she could secure. Scarlett didn't see the point. COVID had turned a full-time job into life itself – no room for relaxation, holidaying, or even visiting. It had become a 24/7 wrestling match against a deadly and unseen opponent.

On one of those nights, she settled herself in front of an electric fireplace in the common room of the hospice. Pulling an eiderdown comforter from a cedar box, Scarlett curled up on the leather couch and watched the rivulets of water race one another down the arched window. Lightning had begun about an hour previous and now the rains had arrived – one of the most common parts of British life she had come to appreciate.

Sleep eluded her, prompting her to rise, put on the electric kettle, and prepare herself some Earl Grey tea. Then she settled into a soft chair by the window and looked out over the darkened grounds, the moist surfaces casting off brilliant diamonds of light whenever the moon broke through the heavy clouds.

She smiled, thinking about how human mortality had more or less dominated her life in recent weeks. Working at St. Anne's, the trip to the Sicilian cemetery, and now a veritable plague moving across the continents like some great scythe cutting down hundreds of thousands of souls. It was as if death itself was in pursuit of her, defining her every moment, inducing darkness where there should have been light.

Quietly, she acknowledged to herself that there were no experts on death – not even hospice administrators. *It's because there's nothing to know about it, just its finality*, she whispered to the rain. Just like those in this blessed residence, everyone approaches death from a position of ignorance. Sure, people react to it in different ways, and perhaps a philosopher or psychologist can make something of that, but, really, one finally approaches it as the great unknown. That's where its terror comes from – like some great mysterious beast below the surface of the water, more capable of crippling the emotions because it cannot be seen.

Death is such a mystery, neither real or unreal. It is but the end of life, its termination. It has no personality, feelings, or affections. This reality has caused writers, philosophers, musicians, and mystics to describe it in metaphors, to try to give it some definition. The list is long, reflecting the inability to truly capture it: pale ghost, dark horse, grim reaper, closed door, last sleep, departed, and, of course, the end. There is literally nothing that one can do to take a path away from it. There is simply no other direction.

Scarlett's eyes wandered to the bookshelves by the fire, populated with hundreds of writings dealing with the end of life experience. She sighed at the thought of death only ever being described from the perspective of the living. The newspapers were full of it, as were the newscasts and social media posts – accounts of those succumbing to a virus that had a name but had little definition.

From the moment someone is born, they begin the process of walking towards death. The young only look forward, simply because the prospect of death is so far off; the elderly look backwards, since death itself is getting too close. Even for herself, Scarlett had to admit, the things that mattered had changed the older she became. The prospect of death actually informed and influenced those changes. Mortality suddenly came into view, casting shade and perspective on what was left of life.

She got up, moving quietly back to the couch, and realized these ruminations were not only too morbid for her, but actually told only part of the story. She had been through enough death to know that it was ennobled by each passing. Empty though death might appear, it was given a dignity with each honoured end of life. She had witnessed enough to know that great souls welcomed death into their midst as though it were a stranger requiring kindness to drive away the fear of the unknown.

Her head leaning back on the embroidered cushion, Scarlett repeated the words of Maya Angelou she had learned by heart in Nova Scotia.

When great trees fall, rocks on distant hills
*   shudder,*
Lions hunker down in tall grasses,
And even elephants lumber after safety.

When great trees fall in forests, small things
*   recoil into silence,*
Their senses eroded beyond fear.

When great souls die, the air around us
*   becomes light, rare, sterile.*
We breathe, briefly. Our eyes, briefly see with a
*   hurtful clarity.*
Our memory, suddenly sharpened,
*   examines,*
gnaws on kind words unsaid, promised walks
*   never taken.*

Great souls die, and our reality, bound to
*   them, takes leave of us,*
Our souls, dependent upon their nurture, now
*   shrink, wizened.*
Our minds, formed and informed by their
*   radiance, fall away.*
We are not so much maddened as reduced
To the unutterable ignorance of dark, cold
*   caves.*

And when great souls die, after a period, peace
    blooms,
Slowly and always irregularly.
Spaces fill with a kind of soothing electric
    vibration.
Our senses, restored, never to be the same,
    whisper to us,
They existed. They existed.
We can be. Be and be better. For they existed.

Scarlett uttered the last sentence as she drifted off. Death was once more vanquished.

11

His weathered hands were chiseling a mortise joint for the lintel over his back door when his remote phone rang. He cursed, until he saw the words on the tiny call display screen: St. Anne's Hospice. He placed hammer and chisel down, and deliberated what to do. He knew it would be Scarlett, but they hadn't communicated since that difficult evening weeks ago at Mulladore. Finally, with a tinge of resignation, he picked up the receiver.

"Bert? It's Scarlett."

To his surprise, he felt a welcome relief. "Well … hello. Yes, how are you, Scarlett?"

He needn't have asked, since he could detect in her few words an exhaustion that sounded beyond fatigue.

"Trying to keep up, as you can imagine," she said quietly.

"Yes, I've been following the news and left a few goodies at your door to pick up your spirits somewhat, but you never collected them."

"I … I haven't been back to Mulladore, I'm afraid," she said in guilty fashion.

"Well, then, that explains it. Are you saying you haven't been home all this time? That explains why I've only ever seen your living room light on. Are you alright?"

"I'm fine," she answered, and he believed her. "It's just a marathon, and through it all I have wanted to call to apologize for the last time …"

"No need for that," he interjected. "That isn't important, given all that you surely must have been through."

He heard a deep sigh at the other end. "That's just it, Bert – it *is* important to me and I'd like to personally apologize. It has hounded me since that awful night and I should have called sooner, I know."

He was at a loss for what to say and, so, remained in silence on his end.

Finally, she asked, "Would you be free for some wine … but only if you're comfortable?"

"Of course. When?"

"Tonight, if possible. I've been commanded to take some time for myself by our board, and it gives me the chance to right some wrongs."

The immediacy of the request actually assuaged his uncertainty. It was clear to him that she valued their brief friendship, and he knew it was reciprocated.

"Tell you what," he began, "I have something of a garden arbour in the back of my property. Why don't I prepare us some supper and take care of the wine? You just bring yourself and we'll see if we can relieve some of the stress and fatigue that you surely have faced." He then added, "Do we need to wear masks?"

"I don't think so, especially if we're outside. Should I come by at eight?"

"No, seven is better," he said good-naturedly. "You'll be tired, and some of the warmth of the day will still linger at that time."

Then, silence. He couldn't tell what was on her mind, or even if she was still on the line. He was about to say something when Scarlett said quietly, "Thank you, Bert. See you at seven."

He stared at the dead receiver, placed it on the table, and returned to his carpentry only to find he had lost interest. Brushing the sawdust and woodchips from his shirt sleeves, he left the tools on the counter and went about gathering the materials for the dinner.

Scarlett appeared at the top of the hour, casually dressed in a cashmere sweater and woollen pants. In her arm she carried a thick book, which she offered to him as she came in the entrance way. Bert flipped it over to examine the front cover.

THE MASTER ARCHITECTURE OF FOURTEENTH CENTURY ENGLAND

A collage of ancient artifacts was displayed on the cloth cover. It was old, very old, he could tell. Opening to the title page, his eyes widened in surprise at the date of publication: 1743 by Witherby Publishing Group.

"My God," he uttered under his breath. "Where did you ever find this?"

"Squirreled away in the attic of St. Anne's Chapel, behind a temporary wall designed to keep one of the eaves from falling in," she answered with a smile.

To her surprise, Bert leaned forward and placed a kiss on her cheek in an action of deep appreciation.

"This is remarkable," he said finally, "but I'm unable to accept it. This belongs in a museum somewhere, or in an attic above an ancient chapel."

They both burst out laughing at the same instant. "Actually, there were three identical volumes up there – all appearing like they'd never been opened.

"Likely one each for the Father, Son, and Holy Spirit," he replied. The ensuing laughter was so spontaneous they felt like they were floating on air from the enjoyment.

He pulled a light jacket from one of the pegs beside the door, motioning for her to follow him out the same door he had been attempting to repair when she had called earlier in the day. Scarlett was delighted to see a wooden table with a ceramic tile top, surrounded by four cedar chairs. On the table was an ornate glass carafe filled halfway with red wine. He motioned for her to sit and proceeded to fill her glass, followed by his own.

"Your dinner is almost ready," he said, before sitting down opposite her and picking up the gift she had just presented him. Thumbing through its pages of drawings and woodcut depictions, he said, "I belong to an architect's association – the Royal Institute of British Architects – and it's doubtful that any of its members would have one of these."

"It's that special?" she asked. "I honestly had no idea. I just thought it would interest you."

"See this?" he said, flipping the cover and showing her the publisher's inscription inside. "Witherby's is the oldest publisher in the English-speaking world. It began in 1740, mostly printing insurance manifests for ships and their cargo. They branched out, becoming a well-known stationer and publisher. Its original owner passed it on to his son, and so on, and so on, for seven generations. It still exists, owned by the Witherby family, only it's now head-quartered in Edinburgh."

"Wow," she responded, looking over the rim of her glass. "How could you possibly know all that?"

He smiled. "Because they produced some of the orig-inal books on English institutional structures and how they were built. Sadly, only a few were likely printed, and it's doubtful any of the Society's members have a copy."

"Except you, that is."

" I still don't feel that I can accept. Plus, I haven't done anything to deserve such a treasure."

"Bert, it's not about that. There are three of these books on ancient architecture upstairs at the chapel and they've likely been there for a couple of centuries, unnoticed by anyone. Please, accept it as a gift to someone with a fine mind for architecture."

He nodded in quiet ascent, his forefinger running over the aged sewn leather binding. Perhaps his neighbour didn't understand how precious the volume was, but even when she learned of its past, she willingly passed it on to him, regardless. It was a special gift from someone he was coming to appreciate.

As the evening air became increasingly infused with a chilly moisture, the two neighbours finished the meal that had produced such delight in Scarlett. "Donair!" she had exclaimed in complete surprise. "How could you possibly know about that?"

"Google," he replied with a smile. When he had first placed the plate of spicy beef and sweet milk-based sauce before her, Scarlett had literally squealed, and dug in without waiting for her host to begin. He had smiled then at her impetuousness and did so again as he watched her finish off the last of her third bowl.

"That is the best thing I have tasted since coming here. Thank you, Bert – what a wonder. It was the last thing I would have expected."

"My pleasure," he said quietly. "Look, let's take our dishes inside and finish our wine by the fire."

After the dishes were put in the dishwasher and the perishables crammed into the refrigerator, they enjoyed the growing comfort of the fire's warmth. Her head was swimming with the three glasses of wine she had consumed. Now she did her best to focus her thoughts on the reason she was there in the first place.

"I know it's too late now to apologize for that evening, but …"

"Scarlett, no matter. It's done; let's move on."

Her countenance revealed her displeasure, but she rallied and said, "Okay, let's do just that – move on. What have you been doing since that awful evening?"

Bert was thankful for the change of subject. "Well, to be honest, not much. The few architectural projects I'm leading are now done by consultation online. All building has been shelved until things either get better or a vaccine is developed. And, so, I've been working around here, doing odd jobs that I should have got to years ago."

He looked directly at her before asking, "But I want to know how you are faring, Scarlett. Following the news, as most of us have, I'm amazed that you are still standing, given all that you are facing. Tell me, can you continue at this pace?"

She placed her head back into the comfort of the chair, the ceiling lights suddenly revealing the depth of her fatigue. He thought for a brief moment that she might have nodded off, but then she swivelled her head to look directly at him.

"I don't mind confessing that I have been in over my head – completely. But so is everyone else it seems, including the government, so I don't feel too overwhelmed. Yet …"

"What?" he asked coaxingly, as he noticed her voice had trailed off.

"I was going to say: Where else would I rather be? These are the urgent days, Bert, days when the fate of humanity lies in the balance. It is times like the present when I am so thankful that I chose the path of healthcare when I was younger. People are afraid, and they require faith in them. That I have lots of, and it feels good. It's as though I must be there for others or else take the word 'compassion' out of my vocabulary. The sooner we realize that caring for each other is a gift in moments like these, the sooner we can get about the business of being human."

He watched her, moved by her assurance in an uncertain time. "Interesting," he responded. "I hardly have your courage or commitment, and I feel a strange sense of alienation. Imagine that, me, the great loner, secure in my solitude, feeling at a loss without people."

Scarlett sat up in an instant. "Bert, is that you in there? I mean, that doesn't sound like the self-assured neighbour I know, albeit briefly."

Certain he didn't have to drive anywhere as the evening progressed, her host rose and grabbed some more wine. He was surprised to realize he wanted to talk, to acknowledge his fight with his emotions. He offered more to his guest, but she simply put her palm over the mouth of the glass. She wanted to be alert and sober for this.

His eyes stared into the fire, lost in thought. His guest would have been surprised to learn that his thoughts were travelling through the streets of 1940 London. He could almost smell the fire and cordite from the explosions of the great Blitz, when Germany dropped 30,000 incendiary bombs on the great capital.

"You should tell me where you are right now, Bert, or else I'll just grow more troubled watching you."

He looked up, smiled genially at her words, and began.

"I was thinking of what my mother told me about the Blitz she endured during the Second World War. My father was in the British navy, somewhere in the Atlantic. She spoke of the fear and dread among her neighbours and friends as the first bombs began to fall. People didn't know what to do, she said. It seemed like everything was ending. And then Winston Churchill toured the ruins and asked people what they were doing in hiding. He encouraged them to get out, go to the dancehalls, dine in the restaurants, go to church, attend the theatre – anything to get life back to normal."

A quiet crept into the room as they both pictured an era where so much seemed apocalyptic. Somehow, through all the gloom and hopelessness, the people of Britain had rallied.

"And why were you thinking of that?" she asked, almost in a whisper. "Why now?"

He looked up and said, "Because I just realized that we can't do any such thing at present. We can't gather. We can't join our voices. We can't console one another. We can't even embrace."

She detected a hint of emotion in his last words. Before she could say anything, Bert added, "For all my years of independence, I find that I miss the human contact. All those things we have taken for granted are gone – for the moment – and all I am left with is myself."

They both drifted into silence and thought. Eventually, he noted her breathing deeply and realized that the wine had at last claimed her. He stirred her until her eyes opened. "Time to go," he urged.

"I'm okay here," she said, her words slurred and weary.

The gentleman in him took control. He helped her to her feet, and with her arm in his, chartered a course to Mulladore. The door was open and he guided her to the couch by the kitchen. She was asleep in a minute. He threw a blanket over her and quietly walked back to his house.

Over and over he considered why he had revealed so much of himself to this woman. It didn't really matter, he concluded, because it felt good to have released those things that had troubled him in recent days.

Instead of going to sleep, he picked up his chisel and hammer, and if Scarlett had been awake, she would have heard his hammer blows on into the night.

12

At some point, four months into the crisis, it had become apparent that the Coronavirus wasn't the only challenge St. Anne's Hospice was facing – the nation's famed health system was under assault.

A second wave of the pandemic, expected and dreaded, moved through the country like a whirlwind, and people, already cowered in fear by the original onslaught, braced for worse to come. People woke up one morning to an alarming BBC report that more than 100 National Health System trusts in England were already at capacity, and that the reality of 10% fewer beds than necessary left the system strained to the breaking point. Some 16,000 beds were required each day in those trusts, and they just weren't available.

It was clear that the system was sagging under the load. When the head of the NHS admitted to the *Guardian* that, "There is insufficient acute bed capacity, and community capacity, to deal with this new demand," it was as if some great secret had been revealed, and what the nation had been sensing for some time was, in fact, true.

It shouldn't have overly surprised anyone. For the last decade and a half the British government had been subtly starving the NHS of required funding, even before the pandemic. The system had been unable to grow its capacity and had been at subsistence levels when COVID first emerged. No one dared to admit it, of course, but hospitals and healthcare facilities were quietly cutting back, unable to meet the demand.

That included hospices, which were especially threatened by the reality that only one-half of their funding came from the NHS; the rest they had to raise themselves. This was never easy, but with the pandemic's presence now raging through the country, hospices couldn't even conduct their public fundraising events due to social distancing measures. Desperation was setting in.

The board of St. Anne's met virtually every week, always online, attempting to sort out the challenges and find a way forward. Already stressed for months by a health emergency no one had seen coming, the meetings had taken on a mild tone of dread. Inevitably, organizers became aware that they would have to consider closing down wings of the hospice just as they were required more than ever. The greatest fear of all was that the building would become a petri dish of COVID itself, forcing it to close down altogether.

One day ran into the next, which ran into the next, leaving all involved with the feeling that time hadn't so much stood still as flattened. The inability to go to school, favourite shops, churches, the theatre, football matches, or even the beach meant that nothing was available to break the monotony of living life in a pandemic. Instead, people read their digital devices endlessly for news of the virus and became glued to their television screens for online movies and television shows. It felt like a suspended world, where so much and so little was happening at the same moment in time.

The board of St. Anne's eventually turned to the subject of possible closure. Other hospices had already made the decision, moving their fragile charges to local hospitals that were already out of space.

"How close are we to making that decision?" Reverend Spelling inquired, his tone slightly raspy.

The board chair sighed and looked around the table. "We are fortunate that we live in a region where many of the older generation retired and brought their saved wealth along with them. Many of their loved ones breathed their last here and their families have faithfully invested in St. Anne's in ways unusual for similar locations." He sighed once more, only this time with an aspect of regret. "As to your question, Reverend, it appears we have, at the most, two months of continuing operations before the decision will have to be made." Observing the expressions on the faces around him, the chair felt more like the Grim Reaper than the seasoned executive he was.

"Then we must prepare for the worst," Lizzie Caufield, the hospice treasurer, said in an almost apologetic tone. "I've been projecting our expense to income ratio over the past few months and we're bleeding funds - not as badly as other hospices, but still serious enough to warrant serious action."

It was as if a collective sigh emerged from the group. It was the moment they dreaded but understood was coming.

It remained for the board chair to launch the discussion and eventual vote on closing down at least one wing of the operation. He opened a small leather binder and scanned the scrawled notes he had earlier jotted down for just this moment. Everyone sensed that some gigantic hammer was about to descend.

"Perhaps there's another way."

The intervention caught them all by surprise and, as one, they turned to face its source.

Scarlett's face reddened at all the sudden attention. Yet she felt neither insecure or intimidated. What she was about to voice was something she had been considering for a week. It had found its origin in a handwritten note she had received from Sandi Templeton's youngest daughter, Elizabeth, not too long after her famous mother's passing. It had been short, but poignant, in its sense of grace and hope.

Scarlett,

My world is still topsy-turvy, set about, as it is, with ensuing bouts of grief and treasured memories. I have come to realize that my mother's end was perhaps even more beautiful than her productive life. She was sad, naturally, but there was a peace in her that I had actually never seen in all the years of knowing her. In fact, as the Bible says, it seemed like a peace that passes all understanding.

I don't know if you ever knew it, but prior to her move to St. Anne's, she dreaded death and any prolonged physical pain that came with it. She had a good life, she knew, but now that the end was approaching, she felt ill-equipped to deal with it. "Imagine that," she observed to me on the way down to St. Anne's for that first time, "my life was just one performance after another, but now that I need to rise to the occasion once again, I can't."

But she did, in perhaps the greatest role of her life. I knew there wasn't one bit of it that was an act or pre-rehearsed. It was all genuine. Any fears that she had were gone. In their place a solitude I have never known my mother to possess. I was amazed — still am.

It has taken me these following weeks to fully realize that it was St. Anne's that was her greatest companion in those final weeks, day, hours. The setting you, your staff, and volunteers set in place transcended anything our family had ever known. Death, when it came, had no opportunity to fill us with dread — it came, performed its historic function, and vanished without leaving any fear in us.

I could go on, but this note is just to say that the peace of St. Anne's lingers with me still and continues to pass all understanding. If our family can ever do anything to assist in paying back the massive emotional debt we owe, please don't fail to respond. We wish to be there for you, as you were for us, and especially mother. Every memory I have of that sanctuary called St. Anne's is good, inspiring, and, yes, healing. God bless all of you.

Elizabeth

Scarlett pulled out that note now and read it in reverential tone. The ensuing silence was sacred and was only accompanied by the odd sniffle. When done, instead of putting the note back in her case, she passed it to the person next to her, who then passed it on to the next. Scarlett waited until it circled back to her, held it in her grasp, and looked around the table.

"Like you, I am fully aware of the challenges this country's hospices are facing. When I phoned my hospice where I previously worked in Canada, I discovered that they are in the same predicament and are in the process of making plans to downsize."

She paused a moment , then began again in a confident tone.

"But that is not our situation. Hard-pressed to be sure, St. Anne's has two factors in its favour. The first is the region where we operate. There is wealth in this southern region of the country, and we are blessed with a well-to-do population of seniors who have come to understand the uniqueness of this building."

Holding the note up before her, she continued.

"And the second reason is found in these kind words of Elizabeth. We know her family has accumulated significant wealth and they will donate generously to us, according to her own promise on this page. But I wish to go further. Younger generations have taken to something called 'crowd sourcing.' It is simply a way of appealing to large segments of a population over the Internet and requesting their help and support of various projects. They set a goal and strive to meet it. Most don't reach expectations, but many do, and it's my belief that such a campaign would secure us the finances required to get us through this crisis. I would like to oversee such an effort, with the help of some local people in the tech industry in and around Dover that I've come to know in my time here."

"I've never heard of such a thing," Marsha Seymour, a

long-serving board member, noted. "You mean you just ask people for money and they just give?"

"Something like that, Marsha. It's all in the messaging and the cause. If you can convince people about the cause, they just go to their computer and donate online. We can set it up so they get their receipt within moments of their gift. The transaction is done without all the expense of our normal financial drives and we can apply the acquired funds immediately."

They had listened to Scarlett's description in silence, intrigued by something they couldn't quite understand but which appeared promising.

Board approval came shortly thereafter, supported in large part because of the trust they had developed in their director's ability and approach, not to mention the personal touch that always characterized her discussions. Everyone departed, feeling a certain sense of hope that hadn't accompanied them when they first arrived for the board meeting.

13

Support for the crowdsourcing campaign had come from an unlikely source: Bert Wynman. Years earlier, as head of the National Architectural Society, he had worked extensively with the British government and a number of emerging digital media companies to develop a vast website to assist the tourism industry to promote famous historical structures in a global campaign.

He had bumped into Scarlett at a local Folkestone market, where everyone was in protective masks, maintaining the appropriate two metres of distance from one another. A chilly wind blew in from the English Channel, carrying papers and bits of scrap along with it, and wound its way through the stalls and narrow passageways, causing everyone to turn up their collars, their heads down against the occasional blast.

Bert spotted his neighbour in a short checkout line just as he was entering. He waited till she was through, not moving until she approached him.

"Bert. O my, I had to do a double-take there. Our masks change everything, don't they?"

"Indeed," he responded, smiling beneath the material covering the lower half of his countenance. "I'm not sure when, or if, our world will ever get back to normal." He waited a moment before asking, "Just in town for some shopping?"

"Same as you I suspect," she said knowingly. "I can't recall the last time I stocked my cupboards, and I'm afraid to look at the various cultures that have grown in my fridge in my absence."

They both laughed naturally, glad to have encountered one another.

"I see you've just arrived," she said. "You'll be happy to know that the French breads and Swiss cheeses are on sale today."

"Maybe a better idea is to grab some tea in the bakery under the atrium over there," he interjected, pointing to the normally popular bistro in the market. "If you've got the time, that is?"

"It would be perfect," she replied.

Ten minutes later they seated themselves at one of the small round tables spaced some distance from the few others in the area. They had two cups of tea and a box of scones before them."

Bert checked his watch, observing, "Actually, we picked a good time to sit down here. The next train through the Chunnel lands here in twenty minutes, and it's likely to get busy." The long tube under the English Channel between Folkestone and Calais, in France, provided a much needed economic advantage to the region.

It was a few minutes later, while on their second cup of

tea, that Scarlett brought up the challenges at St. Anne's and her intention to crowdsource.

"Really," he responded, eyebrows arched in surprise. "What a terrific idea, although I'm not sure the older settlers around here will even know what the term means."

"I know; I thought of that," she said. "Do you remember Sandy Templeton's stay with us a while ago?" He nodded. "Well, her daughter, Elizabeth, has promised the help of their family foundation. I thought I would use that brand, and Sandy's remarkable legacy that still lingers, to entice the older folks to consider investing in St. Anne's as we endure this pandemic."

"Makes sense," he affirmed, placing some jam on his scone. "But what about the younger ones? It's doubtful they even know of Ms. Templeton's effect on her generation."

"I know," Scarlett replied, a tinge of exasperation in her tone. "That's where the crowdsourcing comes in - at least I *hope* it does. I'm a little out of my depth in that area, although I did witness some successful campaigns using that tactic back in Canada."

"Where will you begin, then?"

And that's how it all began - with a simple question that was to have profound effects. It turned out that Bert's contacts were proficient in the advanced techniques of fundraising, especially through the means of social media.

"Have you heard of *Only Progress*?" asked Bert.

She shook her head side to side, prompting him to continue. "It's actually set up in Dover but run by a group of remarkable young women - all of them brilliant - who graduated from respected British universities like Cambridge and the London School of Economics and opted to start their own groundbreaking tech firm, with an eye towards the improvement of humanity. I worked with them last year and was fully unprepared for how gifted they were."

"What … what are you saying? That I should ask them to help?"

"Not exactly," he responded with a smile. "I think we should both visit them. I'll make the introductions and break the ground, while you pitch all the marvels of St. Anne's."

It turned out that the two co-leaders of *Only Progress* were free three days later. Bert picked Scarlett up at the hospice mid-morning and headed east to Dover, shunning the A2 carriageway and taking the more scenic coastal road that tracked over the famous white cliffs before descending into Dover proper.

The location's small population of 31,000, beautiful beaches, and quaint structures drew an endless stream of tourists each year. Visits had been cut in half in recent months, as the pandemic hindered pleasure travel across the country and from the continent.

They spotted the sign for *Only Progress* close to the centre of town, on the second floor of a traditional-looking structure on Biggin Street. Met by an efficient-looking receptionist, after climbing a flight of circular stairs, they were eventually introduced to Penny O'Keefe, a pleasant pixie of a woman, short in stature but tall in personality. Her blonde hair was cropped but feathered in attractive fashion, and her ice-blue eyes looked alive with energy and curiosity.

"I've been looking forward to this encounter," she said, in words as genuine as they were pleasant. Before they could express their own thankfulness, their host noted,

"Both my grandmother and grandfather passed away there, you know - at St. Anne's. They went in a week apart and died on the same day six weeks later. Those were weeks I'll never forget. St. Anne's was our home for that entire time. They were placed in the same room and we were allowed to stay in the ante-room adjacent to theirs. The care was something that lingers with me still and the end, when it came, was one of the most peaceful experiences I can remember. So, yes, *Only Progress* wants to help in any way we can because I guess we are part of your story."

Scarlett pushed back the tears. This was so unexpected that she had no words. She had come with Bert to make her case, but St. Anne's had already done that for her.

Someone brought a series of plates with individual lunch wraps, bottled water, and foil wrapped chocolate wafers. "I thought we'd have some lunch, COVID-style," Penny said through a smile. " No need for masks here if we can keep this distance. Oh, and I've ordered us some tea and coffee."

It turned out that their hosts had much more prepared than just a meal. Penny called in her team and they laid out some designs for a crowdsource campaign based upon the essential strength of St. Anne's Hospice.

"Here are the key steps that we feel make a logical progression as we work through the campaign," she noted.

Before them she put two pieces of paper with five bulleted points:

- how will we do it?
- how will we promote the campaign?
- how will we strategize our outreach?

- how do we manage the results and measure success?
- how do we produce the final project?

"They are all posed as questions," noted Scarlett.

"That's because we need your input." This came from Stephanie Downs, who introduced herself. She was a graduate of Cambridge, and was well-trained in strategic research.

"You mean that we design it?" Scarlett inquired, a bit nonplussed.

Bert reached over and touched her arm. "I think that's exactly what is meant," he said.

"Crowdsourcing isn't just about money being sent in for a cause or a campaign, but ideas as well. Those who donate have the right to participate in the campaign. It's the one key condition of such a venture."

"I don't think I could have put it better," Penny chimed in. "This will become a virtual field of ideas and suggestions, but, in the end, the key ideas have to be yours. We have ideas, naturally – that's our business - but you are at the ethical centre of this work, Scarlett, and your suggestions - what you envision - will drive this work."

Suddenly everything became quiet. "Let me consider this for a moment," she suggested. "And in the meantime, can you explain more fully to me this concept of crowdsourcing? I am acquainted with it, naturally, but you are the experts, and I'd like to know the possibilities."

For the next fifteen minutes, Penny's team went through the essentials of crowdsourcing, how it was a recent phenomenon, and how it had changed the game when it came to fundraising on a grand scale.

Crowdsourcing was the practice of utilizing the wisdom of a group for a common goal. As Bert had implied, those donating didn't just put forth money but also suggestions and concepts. It was a way of solving complex problems in an innovative way by streamlining the flow of information in both directions. The practice had actually existed for centuries, but the digital revolution had the ability to take the concept globally.

In order to be truly successful, organizers had to first break a larger project up into individual micro-tasks. Workers then came together to take on those tasks, speeding up the entire process and reaching goals quickly.

And there were many advantages. It increased the capacity of socializing, especially on the Internet. Large projects suddenly became not only manageable but communicable. It filled the inevitable knowledge gaps with an open and shared sense of knowledge and experience. It empowered community engagement, bypassing traditional marketing procedures and directly approaching those who might be interested in donating.

In a surprising development, crowdsourcing had effectively raised funds for providing protective equipment like ventilators, masks, and shields to frontline workers in the COVID pandemic - raising funds that governments couldn't. It's time had come and was now being employed not just for business causes but for humanitarian good.

That finished, those around the table grew quiet, leaving Scarlett with the unmistakable impression that the floor was now hers. It was now her time and, strangely, she was ready.

"The history of St. Anne's is really one of south England's history. People who lived through some of this country's greatest challenges have passed on to the next stage of their journey in our building. They have taught school, fought in conflicts, explored the world, healed ailing bodies, brought up children and grandchildren, developed their communities, officiated over the birth of the European Union on Britain's behalf, entertained millions, even been into space. They have been who we are - south England's essence.

"It is inevitable that St. Anne's is linked to the subject of death - it's who we are. But those passings represent history, a legacy of our civilization's progress. Most of them weren't luminaries or people of great note, but they built our nation in one way or another. Perhaps most importantly, they chose to live their final hours in this land - not just in England, but at St. Anne's. We are the repository of their remarkable lives. Their influence still lingers in our hallways, dining room, and offices long after they have gone. And now we run the danger of losing that hallowed space of memory and of life because of another great hurdle, global in scope and invisible, that challenges us once more to think differently, to apply a new kind of courage to help us transcend our troubles."

Scarlett stopped to study her hands, her mind searching for the right words. When she finally looked up, it was to gaze directly at everyone around the table.

"St. Anne's is not only beloved by the families who passed through there but by the hundreds of thousands who live in the vicinity and who view it as a legacy of their own care and humanity. I believe we should make the pitch to them to ensure that it continues - not for our sakes, but theirs. We might not be as ancient as Canterbury Cathedral or Dover Castle, but our structure is the testimony of this generation's will to survive, to carry on the great story of our people and their exploits. The residents of this region already feel that in their bones; now it is time to bring their collective conscience to St. Anne's, helping them realize that by saving their hospice we are saving their legacy."

She could have said more, yet sensed it had been enough. Around the table, no one stirred or said a word. Penny O'Keefe permitted the tears to run down her cheeks, making no effort to wipe them away. And when Scarlett looked at Bert, she could see nothing but ... what was it - admiration?

"A new kind of courage, you say," Penny said, finally. "Well, we're in. You have just given us a vision, a rationale, a reason to believe, and a willingness to act. It's more than we could have expected, and it is enough. The rest is just strategy. Now, let's get started."

14

There was no press conference or in-person interviews, but the launch of the initiative took place two weeks from the day Scarlett and Bernie had traveled to Dover - a record turnaround abetted by the advance preparation Only Progress had done.

It was Penny who had come up with brand name *CrowdCare* - an easily recognizable term that embellished both the crowdsourcing and palliative care aspects of St. Anne's. The website CROWDCARE finalized just two days before the launch. Scarlett decided to hold a video launch at the front door of the hospice, surrounded by board members, staff and volunteers. Media and other officials were to tune in online.

But present with Scarlett was Elizabeth Templeton and some of her family members, all wearing masks and prepared with a cheque of £500,000 for presentation. Not all of this money had come from Sandy Templeton's estate, but from well-endowed supporters and fellow entertainers who had been touch by her life over the decades.

It was a wonderful start. Scarlett had gone through how people could donate through the crowdsourcing campaign and Only Progress had arranged a number of online input portals that allowed donors to say what they would like to see done with their money or any ideas they might have had for the hospice.

By midnight of that first day, over £1,000,000 had been offered to the campaign, half of which had come from the Templeton initiative. For a day that had started with no money yet collected, it had had grown into some kind of miracle. Board members who had been at the announcement in the morning and who had fretted over the survival of St. Anne's were dumbfounded by what had unfolded. They knew nothing of crowdsourcing, but its efficacy was immediately obvious and they quietly thanked their lucky stars that Scarlett had been brought on as their leader.

Within in a week it had become clear that the financial crisis for St. Anne's was over, at least for the immediate future. Staff vulnerable to being let go were assured of ongoing employment. Hospice beds were kept open at capacity instead of being closed down for a lack of resources. Even extra clerical staff were hired on a temporary basis to ensure that all the proper criteria for COVID financial accounting were maintained and that St. Anne's remained in compliance with national and local health guidelines. As pressure-filled as these days were, in ironic fashion life was becoming easier at the hospice. Bills were paid on time, resourced sourced and procured, the doors remained open and those in their final months, weeks and days remained the focus of all hospice activities.

A highlight became a special variety event put on by the regional BBC service and produced by Sandy Templeton's family. They had reached out to those in the entertainment industry - authors, musicians, actors, even movie stars - and most agreed to appear in an effort to raise funds for that organization that so looked after their associate and friend Sandy in her final weeks.

Unable to gather physically, the BBC encouraged people to take part in the live performance, both on traditional television and online. Virtual tickets were sold. Memorabilia, like Sandy Templeton CDs and paraphernalia were donated to the cause, sponsors signed on and BBC committed to turning the evening into a special documentary movie to be played repeatedly over the coming months.

And from the moment the donation platform was posted online, supporters came forward in waves. The performance, though live, nevertheless was completed in its 90-minutes time slot, ending just in time for the evening national network newscasts.

As the event closed, Penny O'Keefe came forward with the news that £1,700,000 pounds had been donated and that a further £730,000 was pledged. Defying health guidelines for a brief instant, Scarlett threw her arms around her new friend as their tears mixed together on their cheeks.

"It's not done yet, you know?"

"What do you mean?" asked Scarlett.

"The regional BBC has committed to re-running the program for the next few weeks, at different times, of course. But we have developed the technology to kick into gear during each airing, so that people can just keep giving whenever they are so moved."

It all meant that all financial worries for St. Anne's were cleared off the table. It also enabled the hospice to have an added portable extension built onto the east wing that would help absorb the heavier demand due to the pandemic.

Late that evening, Scarlett arrived at her Mulladore front entrance to find a large bouquet of two dozen roses, accompanied by three bottles of expensive Sauvignon in a straw basket, on the stoop. There was a note that read,

Knowing you, you're likely to finish these in one night. Should you want to celebrate your most wonderful accomplishment, just put your porch light on. I'll be by promptly. Success deserves company. Bert.

She had desired a lengthy bath when arriving home, but Bert's kindness brought a smile to her lips. She picked up the basket, unlocked her door, then placed the wine on the counter. Returned to the front door, she gathered the roses in her arms and switched on the porch light.

Fifteen minutes later she heard the gentle knock at the door and raised her voice, bidding him enter. He smiled at her - a grin which widened the moment he saw the two full wine glasses on the table before her.

"You're set, I see," he said.

She nodded before saying, "It's been a whirlwind, hasn't it Bert? And I'm not forgetting that it was you who initially suggested Only Progress, and Penny."

He sat opposite, sighing. "To be honest, I had no idea that her father had passed away at St. Anne's. That was just serendipity. But I watched her face as you spoke in her office that day and I could see that you had her onside from the beginning."

"She's special."

"That she is," he responded, leaning his head back into the chair padding. "But it has been you, Scarlett, that brought it all to life. You really are a remarkable person and a very able communicator. I like the moniker "CrowdCare" and it serves its purpose. Yet it was how put St. Anne's squarely in the path of history. You're gathering of all the great British moments and placing the hospice in that prestigious company was brilliant, just brilliant."

She didn't reply, embarrassed at his praise. Nevertheless, she was secretly pleased and hoped it didn't show. Scarlett had seen the campaign as a kind of "Hail Mary" pass, a desperate lunge into the unknown. That it has turned out as it did was an overwhelming surprise. It spoke to the power of the public once its collective conscience was enabled. It was rare, to be sure, but what it expressed itself, the national will was more powerful than any government or army.

"Well, you'll be interested to know that I received a telephone call from the vice-president of marketing for the British Broadcasting Corporation," she said, breaking the silence.

"My God, if it's the BBC from London, then it has to be about something national," her guest responded.

"Indeed. The success of CrowdCare and the obvious potential of Sandy Templeton's legacy has them asking if I would agree to something much bigger than what we just had."

"Like what?"

"The actually want to do a physical show. O, the venue will be empty, but the entertainers will be on a literal stage, performing live. They believe it will raise tens of millions of pounds and will be just the thing to distract the country from its COVID troubles. It will be on almost every television and digital screen in the entire UK."

Bert tipped the edge of his near empty glass in her direction. "Well, I can only salute you, my friend. You captured the country's imagination is a way I could never foresee. My suggestion would be that you get your board to consider starting a foundation for St. Anne's."

"What? Why?"

"Because the money about to accrue to you will be significant enough that you can build a permanent funding scheme for the hospice, simply by living off the interest of all those funds."

"I'm thinking about something different," she said, her words now slightly slurred due to the wine and the fatigue.

"Uh, oh, this could prove interesting". He rose, went into the kitchen and returned with an uncorked bottle. "What could possibly be better than saving the future of St. Anne's? he queried, filling her glass.

She looked up at him before saying, "The future success of the entire hospice movement in the country."

Bert wasn't fully sure what she was speaking about, but something in her tone, in the smile that extended to her eyes, provide him a hint of what was coming. He lifted his glass to her and called out, "Here's to spreading all that goodwill … and the money."

Scarlett merely nodded, already thinking of what she would suggest to her board in the morning.

15

They were in a delighted mood a week later as they met in the makeshift boardroom at St. Anne's with their special visitor from the BBC. Anne Wishington had been with the national broadcaster for years, assisting in its transition from regular television, to cable, and, more recently, to digital and online programming.

Scarlett had impressed upon the board a sense of urgency in the need for a meeting, and they had accommodated. Though the members had a surprise in store for their guest, Scarlett was intrigued to note that they gave no indication of anything irregular.

Wishington spent the next half-hour going over the proposed plans the BBC headquarters in London had put together. Ultimately, their key interest wasn't so much the hospice itself but the hope and good news they thought it would bring to the British people in another one of their darkest hours. When she had concluded, she closed her folder and looked around the table, waiting for a response.

Rev. Spelling had been asked to deliver the news and began with a dignified restraint that Scarlett always found so appealing.

"Thank you, Amy - if I may call you that - for this exciting proposition. We are still attempting to get used to the fact that the BBC would take such an interest in our tiny little corner of south England."

"Well, it's not so 'tiny' anymore, Reverend. We've received messages from all over the kingdom, pressing for more information. That's part of what helped us to make the decision to air a program."

Spelling smiled at this confirmation, but moved on.

"We believe it to be a wonderful concept, and your idea of providing hope in a bleak time finds a resonance in all of us here. However, we were wondering if you would be open to one key suggestion that wouldn't affect your programming so much as its recipients?"

Wishington, despite her professional demeanour, nevertheless looked around the table in surprise. "Go on," she said.

"We are a fortunate hospice, living in a country where most of our sister organizations are having to consider either cutting back their operations or closing, at least for a time. Indeed, we were in that position before the generous combined efforts of the BBC and Sandy Templeton's family assisted in pulling us back from the brink."

He paused to take a swig of his coffee, leaving their guest to use that moment to prod: "What is your proposal then?"

The old cleric took no offence at the urgency, perhaps tinged with frustration, in her tone.

"We would like to see the benefits from your program go into a general fund for all hospices across the United Kingdom - that includes Scotland, Wales, and Ireland. We are a charter member of Hospice UK, and it is through that network that we have learned of the deep struggle faced by the hospice movement across the nation. It's a national charity, and, since BBC is our national broadcaster, we wondered if it wouldn't be a better fit to use the special program to highlight a national challenge."

Spelling could have gone on but felt it important to put the idea on the table, simply and with no ambiguity, to see if there would be any initial openness from the broadcaster.

Anne Wishington permitted her gaze to move around the table, studying the faces while still having a certain confusion reflected on her own. Eventually, her eyes settled back on Rev. Spelling.

"So, you're saying you are willing to forego the sizeable returns that would inevitably come to your organization in favour of spreading the goodwill and sharing the funds with other hospices across the country? Do I have that right?"

"Yes. Hospice UK has 210 members across the land and we believe it would send a strong message during this pandemic that we are all in this challenge together for the vulnerable in the entire country, and not just in Kent."

A moment's silence ensued, with every person around the table lost in their own thoughts about the proposal. They all understood the urgency of the moment and its scope. To their surprise, their guest permitted a large smile to spread across her stately features.

"I find this delightful, since we had this discussion with our head office people just yesterday. It had been mentioned that this would have been better suited to a national appeal, but we understood the importance of Sandi Templeton's relationship to St. Anne's, and we didn't want to violate that connection. So, we decided to just concentrate on England's southern shore. We just naturally presumed that it's what you would prefer, and in doing so we underestimated your resolve. I apologize. We should have discerned that people in your line of work, facing death square on, would have a broader empathy than most."

No one said a word, but it was almost as if a collective sigh filtered across the wooden paneled expanse. The concern over how Spelling's proposal would be received evaporated in an instant, in its place a quiet sense of relief and satisfaction.

Wishington had entered the session with a keen desire to broaden the initiative to all parts of the UK but no intent to act on it. This was St. Anne's moment and anything the BBC did would concentrate on that operation. But without one single word or indication from her, they had already embraced the idea, prior to her arrival. They were a special group, she realized, forged together by faith, commitment and, yes, death.

She held up her hand to say just one more thing and the conversation around the table hushed.

"I came here with one special ask, and it still remains important to us at the BBC. We would request that you speak at the conclusion of the broadcast." Her eyes landed squarely on Scarlett, not in some kind of pleading way but with assurance registered in the gaze.

"Me?" Scarlett said, as if in disbelief.

"We watched a video of your reflections at the recent

benefit, and in discussions with *Only Progress*, we have come to the conclusion you have the best way of framing the issues and putting a deeper humanity into the appeal. I watched it a few times actually and came to realize that your words aren't so powerful in asking for something but in giving hope. We will discuss this with Hospice UK to get their approval. I'm sure they have their own spokespeople, but we want you, and I don't think it is too much to ask, since we are taking it national."

Scarlett looked around the table and saw the pleasure emanating from the faces she knew so well. She wanted to fight back on the request until she realized that it was what she wanted. Death and life, experience and innocence of spirit had prepared her for a moment such as this, and Scarlett had felt more empowered and useful in the past number of months than she had in all her life.

She looked over at Wishington and, smiling, merely nodded in assent. A quiet applause filled the room.

"Good," their guest interjected. "Now would it be possible to get some more tea?"

Shortly after the sun set across the wooded lands around Mulladore that evening, Scarlett walked across the road, through to Bert's gate, and knocked on his door, excited to tell him the news. Oddly, there was no answer, even though the lights from both his kitchen and living room were permeating the growing darkness. She walked down the side path to knock on the rear door when Bert called out. Walking around the corner to the front once again, she saw him with his hand up against the door jamb and running his hand through his dishevelled hair.

"I'm sorry, Scarlett, I must have dozed off."

She suddenly saw the fatigue in his face and the droopiness in his eyes. "Are you alright? It's a bit early for a snooze, isn't it?"

He smiled in that kind way he always did. "Yes, I have no excuse. A lot going on lately, and I guess it finally caught up with me." His eyes focused on the limestone slab at their feet, which had become slightly blurry to him.

Finally, he looked up and asked, "Why don't you come in for a drink? Are you hungry; I can throw something together?"

"No, I think you should head to bed. Are you ill, Bert?"

He shook his head to each side. "Just suffering a bit of fatigue, I suppose."

"Well, my friend, I just wanted to tell you that the BBC agreed to the suggestion of having the benefit performance for the purpose of helping all hospices everywhere in the UK. They were actually more open to it than we could have imagined."

Despite the fatigue, the smile that crept across Bert's face filled his neighbour with a kind of joy that had been rare in recent months. It was a smile of such genuine humanity and understanding that it induced her to shift forward and give him a gentle hug.

"Much of this is due to you, you know. Once *Only Progress* came on board, things just took off. And it was you who made that connection."

"I don't think I've ever made a better suggestion in my life," he said through an appreciative smile.

"Look, get some sleep and we'll talk about it all tomorrow. I just wanted you to know first thing."

Bert only nodded and closed the door as she walked around the corner to the gate.

Scarlett should have felt a sense of appreciation and

fulfillment but instead was aware of a sense of concern she was feeling. Bert didn't seem himself at all. When, late that night, she noted that his lights were still on, she knew instinctively that he had gone back to sleep with little thought to household duties.

"Odd," she said quietly.

16

____

The Royal Albert Hall was one of Britain's most venerated structures. Located on the northern edge of South Kensington, London, it had been held in trust for the nation and managed by a registered charity. Being built by the Royal Engineers in 1871 and opened by Queen Victoria, it became one of the favourite venues of the royal family and prestigious entertainers from around the world.

The classically rounded structure was normally home to some 400 events a year, everything from rock concerts to classical performances. But not this season. The venue had been closed for the duration of Covid-19. But for this instance, largely inspired and funded by the BBC, it was opened up for a short 90-minute performance for the country's many hospices.

Everything about it was intimate and carried a natural stillness, partly induced by the plush seats and heavy drapes. The acoustics were perfect and the stage small. Though it once sat some 12,000 people, it now fit 5,000 more comfortably.

Scarlett and Bert had been shown to their seats near the front. She craned her neck to look around, struck by the scarcity of audience members and by the empty private boxes scattered about the higher portions of the side walls.

But there was one that was occupied. Scarlett looked up and across from where she was sitting. Seated alone in the premiere box situated almost over the front edge of the stage were Prince William and Kate Middleton, the Duchess of Cambridge. She went to pull at Bert's elbow but saw that he was already looking in the same direction.

I heard this was possible," he said, not quite in a whisper.

"What do you mean?"

"Well, the Royal Family is the patron of many important British institutions, Hospice UK being just one of them. While the Queen and Prince Philip remain isolated at Balmoral Castle because of the pandemic, William and Kate, along with Charles and Camilla, have taken on royal duties. I heard that Kate Middleton had requested that she and her husband be slated for tonight's performance. Their presence here guarantees that this becomes a premiere event in the BBC universe." Bert paused for a moment, permitting a smile to spread across his face. "And they will be able to hear you. That's quite an honour."

"Yes, it is. Hope I don't get nervous."

"I wasn't speaking of you, but of them," he said, leaving most of his smile to linger on his features. "They are lucky to hear of the hospice movement from someone who has done so much to help it cope in this dark time."

The discussion was interrupted by Anne Wishington. With an official BBC personnel card hanging from her long neck and a navy blue mask covering the majority of her face, she knelt down and said, "So, you two enjoy the performance, but when it comes close to your time Scarlett, one of our assistants, or maybe I, will come to get you to guide you to the proper spot beside the stage. That okay?"

Scarlett nodded and realized that until that moment she had been perfectly calm. Now, she felt a slight churning in the pit of her stomach, though she did her best to remain placid.

"Don't fret about it," Bert said, watching Wishington's form disappear behind a curtain. "How long do you have?"

"Five minutes, they say."

"Well, then that's hardly long enough to cause you any worry," he said, his hand lightly touching her forearm. He looked at her hand, asking, "What, no notes?"

Scarlett sighed. "As you say, hardly enough time to worry about" - an observation that brought on a shared bout of laughter.

A moment later the lights dimmed, and two figures, well-known to all of Britain and beyond, walked briskly to centre stage. One was a seasoned Shakespearean actor who had transitioned to a movie career seamlessly. The other was a young woman who was in the process of gathering fame for her complex performance in a BBC miniseries, playing a young police inspector on the trail of a modern Chinese spy.

They were perfect together - slightly intimate, respectful, and, as would be expected, articulate. Each bore marked accents: his the lake district English, and hers the slight accent of Newmarket Scottish.

The producers had deliberately opted to pace the performances rather than cramming as much talent into the 90 minutes as they could manage. This led to a subtle variety of entertaining moments, suitable to the theme of the evening. There was singing, instrumentals, and a hilarious performance by Mickey Sakes - England's top comedian. He played the part of a man thinking he was entering a hospice when in fact he was in a clinic performing colonoscopies. As he played every movement to precision, the small audience erupted into endless bursts of laughter and clapping.

At some point - Scarlett didn't know how long - the Duke and Duchess of Cambridge emerged through the central opening of the huge curtain, holding hands, and looking fully comfortable together.

Sincerely charming was the most apt description of the aura the two regal figures projected. They spoke eloquently of Queen Elizabeth and Prince Philip, what they had endured through years of war, and the resilience they had demonstrated for the British people. Many of that generation were, sadly, now in their final years, and the nation owed them everything. But it was more complicated than that, for people of all ages were spending their final moments in the hundreds of hospitals across the country.

"These are our fellow citizens," the Prince said gently, "and they deserve all the care and compassion we can give them. The UK Hospice movement needs your help and Her Majesty, Queen Elizabeth, asks that you consider donating to this most human of our institutions."

The stage had been set for a collection of Britain's most famous singers to assemble, socially distanced, to offer a moving rendition of "That's What Friends are For," written by Burt Bacharach and Carole Bayer Sager. The subtle movements of the performers, gliding comfortably around one another without getting too close, succeeded in making it a wonderfully sensitive rendition.

Scarlett had been lost in its effects when Anne Wishington suddenly appeared, beckoning for her to follow. Bert placed his hand on her shoulder and said, "This is going to be the most memorable part of the evening for me. Well done, Scarlett. Well done." She rose from her seat, unexpectedly emotional.

Standing alone in front of an almost empty chamber could have unnerved her, but Scarlett instinctively understood that cameras, moving about her and intersecting at different angles, were her true audience for this special evening. For beyond them lay the loyal 20 million BBC viewers in Britain and the millions of other both at home and on the Continent, along with a global Internet audience tuning in to see the famous performers. With a confidence that was genuine, she spoke to whichever camera had its red light displayed at its front.

The final scene of Christopher Nolan's epic tale, *Dunkirk*, follows a Spitfire pilot who has saved hundreds of our soldiers on the beach through his skill but who, through that willing sacrifice, runs out of fuel and is forced to land on the beach. The rest watch him, understanding his significance, and the fact that he is now alone, having served his nation with all the bravery he could muster. It is as moving as any five-minute length of film and reminds us what has been expended just so that we, this diverse and special people, can still serve humanity, rounding off its rough edges and introducing refinement and history to the human journey.

Tonight, as we enjoy these wonderful performances, hundreds of our fellow citizens are on their final flight as well. Can we lift our eyes and see them? They have saved us, served us, enriched us, instructed us, and bettered us. We live because they lived and built. But they are out of fuel, their frail human frames near exhaustion.

They are surrounded by family and friends, and now a grateful nation. We wish to ease their passage to the life that comes next, even as we go about our daily tasks. Thanks to these wonderful performances, and the insightful words of our own royal family, we now see them, and our hearts fill with respect just as our eyes fill with tears.

On this final flight, they are surrounded by some of the most qualified, caring, and sacrificial people that this country possesses. Thousands of them are volunteers. Many are family members suddenly turned into caregivers of the best sort. They carry on the great tradition of this land's hospice movement. Most of the hospices in England, Wales, Scotland, and Ireland were started in communities without receiving any government support. And they ended up becoming the grand final staging point for our citizens whose time has come to venture on.

The UK Hospice network is quietly turning this nation into a more compassionate people - a people capable of remembering who we are, ready to face what comes next. Some of our finest people will pass on even as this performance concludes, but thanks to Hospice UK, they will be sent on their way through the best wishes our humanity can confer.

Sandi Templeton knew this, experienced it, lived it,

and paid it forward. She reminded us in her final days in a hospice that each of us will die when our time comes, but that the goal is not to live forever, but to create something that will. If anyone understands this it is the people of the UK. Those great gifts of jurisprudence, of drama, industry, invention, medical care, language, freedom from subservience, and so much more are the endowment of this great people to the human race. They came through sacrifice and the understanding that what we build endures long after we have left here for our next stage in life.

Those who pass each day in any of our hospices have left us the world we now enjoy. Our task, now, is to remember them: to look up into the sky and thank God for the very memory and accomplishment they instilled within us.

Please support UK Hospice. In doing so, you not only make the final days of some very fine people comfortable and hopeful, you confer on them the legacy of builders and sustainers of our greatest achievements. A generation is passing. A generation is being born. Let us all help in making a respectful transition.

It was over before anyone realized it. Scarlett simply bowed slightly and headed off to the side of the stage from the direction she came. She could hear the scattered applause and the muffled sounds of the two hosts for the evening, and then she discerned the concluding pre-recorded philharmonic sounds, signalling that it was over. Before anyone could speak to her, Scarlett descended the low flight of stairs and took her place next to Bert. Anne Wishington appeared from nowhere, a broad smile on her face. She looked down at her special guest.

"That was perfect, Scarlett - just perfect. And I think it was perhaps the shortest speech we have heard at one of these events. Entertainers tend to go longer than scheduled."

"That's because I'm not an entertainer," Scarlett said through a gentle smile.

"Perhaps," her host nodded, "but you are a communicator, a gifted one. You ended the evening on just the right note, and your depiction of the generations paying homage to one another was just the right touch. Thank you Scarlett."

Bert and Scarlett remained seated for a few minutes, taking in the importance of the evening and the grandeur of the venue in which it occurred. They had both looked up to the Royal Box in the same instant, but the Duke and Duchess had already departed, whisked away by security personnel.

"She was right, you know," Bert said quietly.

"Who? Anne?" she asked, turning to face him.

"You are a gifted communicator, just as she said. Did you know that the civilian fleet that sailed over to rescue our soldiers stranded at Dunkirk departed from near the white cliffs?"

"I did. That's in part why I mentioned it."

Bert sat back, sighing. "See, you are a storyteller, and the story you spoke of tonight likely moved a vast audience." He paused briefly before noting, "And I timed it, you know. You took two of your allotted five minutes. You were remarkable."

Scarlett looked over at him, smiled, and placed her hand on his shoulder. She felt fulfilled.

Scarlett had known she couldn't have handled the drive from London to Mulladore after a late evening, and had persuaded Bert to take the two rooms offered them by the BBC at the Pelham Hotel, two streets over from the Royal Albert in South Kensington.

Now, as she lay back on the queen size mattress with its luxurious coverings and pillows, she permitted herself to reflect on the evening and its success. Her eyes followed the eight-foot high headboard up to the ceiling cornices and she remembered the first moment of looking up into the various balconies at the Royal Albert. The stage had seem small, but she knew this only added to the intimacy in what had become a delightful evening.

Visitors spoke effusively of her speech backstage, with the producer noting that her speech had taken two and one-half minutes instead of the scheduled five. "It's not often we finish early, but your speech was poignant, and didn't require excessive length." She had liked that. Normally, the royal couple would have remained briefly behind, but COVID restrictions saw their handlers whisking them out of the theatre and into the waiting Jaguars before most people realized they had departed.

Scarlett now understood that any financial worries about St. Anne's were over, for the next few years at least. All the exposure had resulted in an overabundance of financial donations, and that was bound to present two key difficulties for the organization. First, how to disburse all that bounty? It was a wonderful problem, but a challenge, and they would have to work their way through the process in the next few months. And, secondly, she knew instinctively that, with all the exposure afforded the hospice movement in these few days, it was inevitable that requests for residence there would mushroom.

Similarly to Canada, Britain and its people knew little of the hospice movement and the strengths it offered to the National Health System. Representing a far more cost-effective option to the palliative care interventions of the nation's hospitals, hospices remained largely under-utilized.

In her time at St. Anne's, Scarlett had come to respect the quality of healthcare in Britain, but it was, nevertheless, a gargantuan machine, consuming vast amounts of government funding. Its reach was vast - primary care, in-patient care, long-term healthcare, ophthalmology, and dentistry. In all this vast array of human care, those in their final weeks and months of life remained far down the priority list.

While hospice care in Britain was free, it was financed by the NHS, but only in part. The rest had to be raised from private donations, and that was where the challenge came in. Hospice care teams included doctors, nurses, social workers, therapists, counsellors, and trained volunteers. That left little time to concentrate on the increasingly professional art of fundraising, especially considering how many other major players were hunting after the same donors.

What it all meant was the nation's hospices were never able to achieve their full potential, and funding was always their main challenge. Some, especially in rural areas, had gone under, since they were too far removed from other health institutions like hospitals, labs, and extra shifts of needed healthcare workers.

Because of its proximity to Dover and the white cliffs, the vast network of retirees, many of them from professional sectors, had permitted St. Anne's to keep its head above water. But as challenges grew, the need for fundraising expertise was becoming more acute.

Which is why Scarlett had always thought it odd that she had been selected to direct the institution, since fundraising wasn't one of her strengths. And now, here she was, responsible for coming up with plans for taking hospice needs to a larger audience through the media, and bringing in millions of pounds in the process. She smiled to herself, appreciating the irony.

It was then that her mind drifted to Bert, who, she could hear, was watching television in the room next door. His quiet professional life had drawn in numerous contacts - people and organizations with an interest in culture and the care of humanity. He had set her on the original path and accompanied her as she entered the ecosystem of the vast BBC world. His quiet observations, vast experience, and steady support had been largely responsible for bringing her to this point.

She allowed her mind to wander, seeking different ways

for recognizing his profound influence on St. Anne's, and now the entire hospice movement. She had passed the phase of feeling guilty for not seeing him for much of the months since she had arrived in England. And when quarantine protocols were put in place, she was often forced to self-isolate with members of her staff, meaning that she didn't even get home for weeks at a time.

And yet Bert had never withdrawn, despite his reserved nature, and had helped out in numerous ways in her absence, tidying her garden, gathering her mail, even cleaning the windows after a particularly violent rain storm. And his advanced carpentry skills had enabled the securing of one of the great beams in the living room to the wall, the pointing of the stonework in the fireplace, the fixing of the back screen door, and even the repairing of a fallen roof shingle. Then there was the occasional bottle of wine and brick of cheese left at her door when he knew she would be coming back home. It was all these little things that had afforded her the opportunity to concentrate on the challenge before her and to just relax when she arrived at her front door at last.

Scarlett waited in the hotel lobby in the morning, refreshed from a satisfying sleep and a long hot shower. For the first time, she noted how empty the place was, due to the pandemic. The Pelham Hotel was a London staple - an immaculately white exterior contrasting with a seasoned dark wooden interior lined with bookshelves and the occasional fireplace. It would have been beautiful with patrons moving through its lobby, but in this strange COVID world it appeared more like a museum – sterile, insensitive to human presence.

She looked down at her FitBit watch, noting that Bert

was almost twenty minutes late – the first time she had ever known him to be tardy. Her attention was summoned away by the sound of clothes rustling near the elevator. Her neighbour rapidly approached her, a harried look on his face, hair unkempt, and beads of sweat visible on his forehead.

"My humble apologies, Scarlett. I slept far too long - most unusual for me."

She placed a hand on his shoulder, thinking he looked odd. Scarlett couldn't quite place it, but he seemed slightly out of step with himself.

Neither possessed a suitcase, so they stepped out onto the street. As Scarlett looped her mask around her ears, Bert looked at her, frustrated. "I'm afraid I left my medical mask in the room," he said, slightly agitated.

"It's okay, I've got a few here in my purse," she responded, handing him one of the faint blue gauze masks that everyone seemed to be wearing.

They waited, enjoying the rays of the morning sun, as the valet brought Bert's car up from the underground lot. Scarlett tipped him before moving into the passenger seat and belted herself in. Bert pulled out easily into the accompanying lane, the traffic mercifully light thanks to the pandemic. His authentic 1960s Triumph Herald sportscar with its 147cc engine, classic as it was, nevertheless had trouble keeping up with the quickly moving A2 traffic. Eventually, he pulled over into the slow lane, settling back at a more leisurely pace.

The next hour was an enjoyable rehashing of the previous night's performance and the implications for the hospice movement nationally and St. Anne's locally. The sun eventually emerged, permitting them to lower their windows, since the Triumph, made in the 1950s, possessed no air conditioning.

"I have a proposition for you, Bert, and I want you to be open-minded about it," Scarlett said, a certain buoyancy in her tone.

"Alright," he responded, eyes firmly fixed on the road before him.

"I believe it's time you joined the board of St. Anne's Hospice. And before you say anything, it's not so much because of all the wonderful service you have done us. It's just that I could use your presence as we navigate our new future. You have become something like a muse for me - sage, intuitive, understanding of the broader world."

"O dear, you need to bone up on Greek mythology," Bert said, glancing over.

"What's that got to do with it?"

"Well, officially, the muses were nine daughters of Zeus, though the person put in charge of them was Apollo. I'd say that's a bit audacious a term for me, don't you think? How about just 'adviser' instead?"

Scarlett couldn't stop smiling at the thought of it all. "No, that's too menial, I think. How about mentor, since it won't be official?"

"No that wouldn't work either. I've actually learned more from you in these last months than anything I may have helped you with. How about just 'friend' as a better term?"

"So, you'll do it as 'just friend?' I'd like that."

Scarlett suddenly grew alarmed as the Triumph almost veered into the ditch, and looking over at Bert she could see he was somewhat disoriented. He geared down and braked slowly until the vehicle came to rest at the side.

Before she could say anything Bert asked, "Do you think you could take it from here, Scarlett? I'm still fatigued from last night and you're likely more alert. Just stay on the A2 and we'll be back in a couple of hours."

The rest of the trip continued in silence, as Bert nodded off, his head slumped into his chest. Occasionally he would raise it to say something, appearing alert, but he inevitably dozed off once more.

Scarlett pulled the car into her driveway, weary from the drive. "How about wine, or even tea?" she inquired.

Her friend smiled in that gracious way of his, but demurred. "Actually, I think I'll try to catch up on some rest. Perhaps tomorrow night?"

She realized, watching him drive slowly across the road, that she had forgotten to thank him one final time. Her gaze followed him as he retreated into the gloom until he became a part of it.

18

Bert's joining with the hospice board wasn't to be. The flurry of activity around St. Anne's higher public profile and the BBC performance had delayed Scarlett's opportunity to speak with her neighbour about his participation. When she finally journeyed across the road to raise the subject, her eyes registered immediate concern over his appearance. She hadn't seen him for two weeks, and the change was dramatic.

"Bert. Bert, what's wrong?" she asked, fearful of the response, her hand rising immediately to his shoulder.

"Please, come in. It's nice to see you."

She followed him into the kitchen, where he slowly moved to switch on the electric kettle for tea. In practiced fashion, she went to the cupboard by the side of the old deep porcelain country sink and lifted out two cups. Placing them on the round wooden table, Scarlett waited for Bert to join her.

When he sat down opposite her, a sigh escaped his lips. Observing closely, Scarlett battled within herself about how to press her neighbour and friend for information regarding what was wrong. Bert took the worry from her.

"I've not been myself for a number of months," he began. "My energy is gone. I don't feel like eating much. And I have developed a series of headaches that must be something like migraines - which I have never had, by the way."

"And you've been to the doctor?" Scarlett asked, pouring the tea from the pot into both their cups.

"I have, and they've put me through a series of tests. I was fortunate actually, since the hospitals and all that medical equipment are at a premium these days with COVID. I think they must think it's serious." When he finished those last few words, Bert looked up at Scarlett and attempted to smile while tears built up around the rims of his eyes.

"Tell me, Bert … just tell me." It was the way they had always been with one another, and she felt the need at this present moment for frankness.

He lifted his hand, pointed a finger, and touched it to the side of his head. "They believe it's a brain tumour, likely cancerous, and expanding."

It felt as though her heart had fallen out of her chest. She remembered his vitality and health when she first met him not all that long ago. Always working with his hands, he had fashioned most of the things in this house they were sitting in. And his life had been an active one, as he toured the various regions of southern England in his role with the architectural association.

But now she realized that the signs were there. Sadly, though understandably, she had been too busy in recent weeks to join the dots - those occasions where he didn't seem himself. Only now did it become obvious: the fatigue, the slurring of speech even before the wine flowed, the occasional mood swing that was so opposite to his steady nature. Yes, they were there and she, for all her training in spotting such things, had missed them. Scarlett felt a sudden nagging guilt.

"Oh Bert, I'm so sorry. I should have spotted the symptoms …".

"And how could you have done that," he interrupted, "when your life has been nothing but hectic with all the BBC things to arrange?"

It was true, she knew. And, more importantly, Scarlett's clear mind helped her to see that he understood and had never made an issue of it. Looking into his tired eyes now, she discerned the truth hiding behind them, like a barely distinguishable shadow. It was bad, she now understood.

"Is it … is it …?"

"Terminal, you want to say?" he interrupted, still smiling. "Apparently it is. Because the tumour is in the dead-centre of my brain, operating is out of the question. It is expanding but they can release some of the pressure. But, alas, my favourite neighbour, the time that must come for us all is now coming for me."

"Chemotherapy?"

"Sure, but it will only delay things by a few months and the effects will be severe. So, no, that won't be an option for me."

Scarlett rose and walked to a sideboard, from which she removed a bottle of Romanee Conti red wine she had given to Bert weeks earlier. It was still unopened. Returning with two glasses, she motioned to the couch before the fireplace. He smiled, lifted himself gently, and joined her.

"Are you sure about it … the chemo, I mean? What about your relatives and architecture associates? Wouldn't they wish for you to linger somewhat, if you can?"

Her host sipped from the glass, prompting her to suddenly grab it. "Oh my, I wasn't thinking. It's probably not the best thing for you right now."

Pulling it back, he remarked, "The doctors haven't said anything about that, actually, and since intervention efforts aren't in the plan for me, I shall choose to consume what I wish." With that, he clinked her glass with his and took his first swallow.

"What about family?" Scarlett inquired.

He rose momentarily and switched on the circuit that produced natural gas flames in the fireplace before answering. "Well, as you know, my brother passed on a few years ago and I virtually never see any of my distant cousins. Since I never married, it makes far less people that I have to say goodbye to - fortunate, I think."

His guest wasn't sure about that at all. "Well, it's been my experience that it's in our moments of great need that our emotional commitments tend to be of great comfort," she observed.

"That presupposes I'm in need of comfort," he countered, with a smile.

They had been in this place before, and always he had deftly moved the discussion in another direction. It had been frustrating, especially for someone who had covered such considerable ground at handling human emotions as Scarlett, but she opted to push again.

"You say that now, Bert, but as time moves on and things worsen, you might not feel then as you do now. The human consciousness tends to desire connection with others whenever it is threatened or isolated."

"O Scarlett, there's that wonderful humanitarian heart of yours rising up again," Bert said before taking a sip from his glass. "The problem is that the situation is already what it is. To have companionship in these final weeks or months means that I needed to have it prior and, alas, I have tended to live my life in solitary fashion, as you well know. I now must face the consequences of those choices, and I feel ready for it. That man who so effectively divided our country, Martin Luther, said during the Reformation: 'Every man must do things alone; he must do his own believing and his own dying.' That's as good a motto for me as any."

She mulled this over while staring into the flames. He was so infuriating when he got like this – always philosophizing as a means of evading reality. And his deteriorating condition called for sympathy, not preaching. She let it go, knowing there would be other days. But her spirit was agitated, nonetheless.

19

____

The next week brought the welcome news that a number of vaccines had received approvals from health agencies around the world for mass production. Britain was fortunate in having two different vaccines at the ready - the first developed by Oxford University and U.K.-based drug maker AstraZeneca, and the second a collaboration between the drug firm Pfizer and the German firm BioNTech. Altogether, over 100 million doses were slated for application in the next three months.

Scarlett met with her staff after the announcement, reminding them that they were still a long way from hospice life returning to some sense of normality - perhaps even a year. Still, the sense of palpable relief infused the hospice environment with a new kind of lightness, despite the nearness of death.

For the first time in weeks, the St. Anne's board gathered physically in a specially cleaned and disinfected room at the rear of the structure. Individual desks had been placed in the enclosure, the properly prescribed distance apart, and a large white smart screen had been brought in and placed at the front of the room.

The chair began the meeting with the acknowledgement of just how much all the members had missed one another in recent months and confirming that video board sessions, fine as they were, couldn't compare to a physical gathering. Everyone nodded and smiled in agreement. He also noted that this was a special meeting and he thought it best that they all gather in the same room.

The minutes and agenda were presented and approved, and then it was over to the Qualified Accountant, Miles Hamish. He proceeded to talk the group through the remarkably altered financial situation of St. Anne's. Only two months before they were on the verge of making some difficult financial cuts, but things had now totally reversed. He itemized each intervention: Sandi Templeton's influence, *Only Progress* and the crowd-sourcing campaign, the local BBC production, and, finally, the notable evening at the St. Albert's Hall.

"We have all suspected that our financial troubles are behind us," Hamish said in conclusion, "but the reality is that we now have £18,430,000 in our savings. And the donations continue to arrive at a pace that could see us double that amount within the next month." He closed his folder before adding, "And in speaking with my counterparts in other parts of the country, they, too, are enjoying the BBC dividend. The entire organization of Hospice UK is in the most stable position it has ever known. The challenge of this next year is to make sure our future plans are sustainable and not excessive."

The room sat stunned. Given the recent positive exposure for the hospice, they had suspected the news would be good. But nothing like this – not even close.

"So, we have some decisions to make concerning how to handle this bounty. How much should we invest? Should we build the new wing we have spoken of? Bring on more staff? These are the questions we must begin the process of answering today."

He left everyone to ruminate on his words before turning to Scarlett. "Our appreciation of your efforts as our Executive Director are deep, Scarlett. When we first made the request for you to join our institution it was with the understanding that, perhaps, you could get us through the transition years that we knew lay ahead. But that was before this pandemic, or Sandy Templeton, or the national attention we have garnered in this last while. It's only right that we seek your input as to how you believe this financial windfall should be invested."

Scarlett had been pondering the matter in recent days, despite the distraction she suffered at the knowledge of Bert's news. She sat up, facing the table, and was about to add her insights when a voice from her right side interrupted. It came from Sara Ravenhill - a long-serving board member whose husband had passed at St. Anne's over ten years previously. They had enjoyed fabulous wealth - a bounty now passed to her in the will. She always said little at these meetings, but her influence was always felt.

"It goes without saying that we, as a board, very much appreciate Scarlett's ability to raise this organization's profile to the extent that we are as flush as we are today. But I find myself wondering if it has come at a cost." She stopped then, clearly hesitant to continue.

"Please, Sara, go on," Rev. Spelling urged. "These

changes of recent months have been so dramatic that we have more often just moved along with things, with little time to examine the developments. Do you feel we are moving down the wrong road?"

Ravenhill was in her mid-80s but was, as always, dressed impeccably, her grey hair tied back in a refined fashion. She had been the product of one of the country's finest women's schools, Sherborne, in Dorset, and she had been married early to Leslie Ravenhill, one of the British architects of the European Union. She had never known want, but she also had no acquaintance with idleness, having served as a patron to many charitable causes. Her husband had been severely injured in an airplane crash - a tragedy that made her invest herself more deeply into the humanitarian causes she loved, including St. Anne's. She was composed, kind and confident - a perfect representative of the old order that once oversaw the affairs of the nation.

"Much of my support for this institution originated from the two months my husband Leslie spent here at the end of his life. It was quiet, reverent, and still - a fitting sacred place. It has maintained that ambience over the years since … until this last year, I fear. While St. Anne's blended into this area like some vaunted structure, always present but not intrusive, in recent months it has become a … a …. well, a noisy place, full of action, and celebrity. I sense it an atmosphere not suitable to the end of life."

No one was expecting this, so no one present had developed a response. "Perhaps you should explain a bit further," Reverend Spelling urged. "These are important points, and it's likely some, perhaps many, in the area hold feelings similar to yours."

The older woman, dignified and attentive, demurred. "I think it likely that I have said enough. I know these are difficult times, but such occasions call for stability, institutional memory, perhaps a degree of history. I apologize if I have disrupted the arc of events here." She then sat back in her chair, hands folded over a tissue she had produced from somewhere, and stared at it.

"Well, it appears as though our recent success has come at some cost" the chair observed after a time. "How do others feel?"

A surprising intervention came from the seat opposite Ravenhill's. Saanvi Nanayakkara's tone was friendly, though slightly strained, as she spoke up for the first time in months. She owned a highly successful clothing apparel chain that had numerous stores across south England. Like Sara Ravenhill, she was dressed immaculately.

"I have lived in the Dover area for the last twenty years, after I came with my aging parents from Sri Lanka. When my father died and I was asked to join this board, I was honoured. Perhaps it is because of my culture, but I have never quite become used to how the UK views death. Other than great moments, like war or the death of a monarch, you view death in such a reverential fashion that it is almost secret. Most funerals in this land go by almost invisibly. I believe that is why all hospices here remain largely unknown."

"Can you explain that a bit further?" Thomas Spelling asked. "This might be a crucial point."

Saanvi sighed in her attempt to find the right words. "One only encounters a hospice during a time of great personal pain, amid the impending loss. It is in those moments, when a loved one can no longer be helped with palliative care in a hospital that the possibility of hospice care is opened up to them. Most have no idea how it functions or even where hospices are located."

"But that only makes sense," Sara Ravenhill interjected. "It's like a church, which most people frequent only for christenings, weddings, or funerals. In those moments, houses of faith become important."

Saanvi looked across the table at the older lady. "You are right, Sara, but is that all churches are for?"

"What do you mean?" Ravenhill asked.

"Well, aren't churches about everyday faith, about life, about honesty and virtue, beautiful music, and refined character. Yes, they are also about death, but seen only in that way they become mere extensions of the graveyards that surround so many of our faith edifices."

Ravenhill appeared confused, so Saanvi attempted to explain.

"In Sri Lanki, people prepare for death for most of their adult life, seeing it as a rite of passage, like births or marriages. When a monk is called to the death bed, the dying person accepts their fate, pronouncing the appropriate religious precepts. Most importantly, the entire family joins in."

"But that is no different from here," Ravenhill observed.

"Yes, that's true, but that's not all there is. Death is something like a glorious play - a celebration of family history and a life well-lived. Once the person has passed, the coffin is returned to the person's home, and for days feasts are held for family, friends and neighbours. On the sixth day after the death, the monk returns to the home and a big crowd is waiting. There is the clear belief that the spirit of the departed is among them, joining in the actions. Then, every three months for a year, people gather once more to remember and honour the spirit of the one departed."

She paused for a moment to look around the table. "The point I am trying to make is that death in my homeland is a very public affair. When a person passes, and for months and years afterwards, the entire community is aware of what happened, and they speak of the soul that has gone as though it remains, communing with the community. It is … It is one of the key tenets not just of our faith but our communal life. It's something I miss here."

It was proof of Sara Ravenhill's refined temperament that she listened to all this with a look of sincere empathy in her gaze. When no one responded to the previous comments, she spoke up.

"I'm from old Britain - the Britain that used to be and no longer is. Saanvi's observations remind me of when I first read Peter Pan, when he observed that to die must be an awfully great adventure. It's true, but my generation made it a private thing, whereas in Sri Lanka it is public … wonderfully so. This country has changed so much since I was young, but I do not resent it. I sometimes fail to comprehend it, but I have no regrets. Every society on earth is now encapsulated within our borders, and I can only imagine that the hospice experience could be enriched by embracing all of them. Death is not a British thing, but a human unfolding."

In a movement that people would remember for some time, Sara reached across the table and firmly held on to Saanvi's hand. "Thank you," she said, almost silently.

That display of humanity assisted the board in recognizing that the raised profile St. Anne's now enjoyed through Scarlett's leadership would likely open up hospice services throughout the country. The more enlightened the public became about it, the more people in their last stages of life would ultimately see it as an alternative to hospital care.

There was just one problem, and it was significant. For a large portion of individual operations in Hospice UK, only a portion of their costs was covered by the health system. The rest had to be raised by the hospices themselves. The present arrangement was fine for St. Anne's, now with its new-found wealth, but most of the others would have to locate new sources of funding to sustain the increase in patients that the new awareness was bound to bring on.

20

Exhausted, Scarlett made her way back to Mulladore with a mixed sensation of fulfillment and a nagging worry concerning Bert.

She felt confident that the board was now primed for what would come next. That was confirmed later in the meeting when Saanvi Nanayakkara was asked to head a special committee to research how the organization might offer its end-of-life services to the various ethnic communities in southern England. In a nice touch, Sara Ravenhill offered her services to the committee, which were immediately accepted.

Nanayakkara had approached Scarlett and Reverend Spelling as the participants filed out of the meeting. "Are you certain St. Anne's is ready for this?" she asked, a twitch in her left eyebrow hinting that she might be nervous.

"Why wouldn't we be?" asked the cleric. "It seems to me that it's a logical step forward."

There was silence for a minute, prompting Scarlett to

145

press further. "What are you thinking, Nanayakkara? What's the concern?"

"Two weeks ago, I took a brief stroll through the hospice in my role as a board member, and it hit me."

"What hit you?" the Reverend asked. "Was something missing?"

"Just one thing, really," she answered quickly enough.

"What?" he asked again.

"Colour – that's what was missing. Almost all of our residents are white and elderly. All of our support staff are white. And the same can be said for our volunteers. In light of our decision at this meeting, I'm left to wonder if we actually have the capacity or the will for the kind of change that will surely come if we adopt a new diversity policy."

The note of urgency in her voice was shared by the other two. To Scarlett, this was an example of how reality can sometimes overwhelm any chance to make real change. Her own country of Canada was officially termed "multi-cultural" and Britain had taken on that label decades before. But, as in France, prejudice and racism were driven deep into the British populace, and were, to some extent, intensified by such policy changes.

"Look, let's head into the kitchen and I'll put on a pot of tea. We need to discuss this, before we go any further down this road." Both women nodded in agreement with Speller's suggestion, and the three shuffled down the corridor towards the small dining area. Nanayakkara and Scarlett watched through the arched windows as their fellow board members entered their vehicles and moved off down the driveway.

The Reverend approached the table with a patterned ceramic teapot and cups before sitting down between them.

As each prepared their cup, he urged, "Tell us what we might be missing in all of this?"

Stirring milk into her cup, Nanayakkara looked up and began. "I have frequently thought that this country's place in history has been so profound that we fail to understand the changes emerging within."

"Other ethnicities, you mean?" asked Scarlett

"Yes, but the cultures this variety of human experience bring to us as well. It was only in the 1960s that immigration began to increase, but there were already significant populations from former empire and Commonwealth nations who had earned British citizenship and had become established in various government departments. But, as new immigrants began arriving, new ethnic communities began emerging, especially in London and the more major centres. This resulted in heightened racist opposition and led to a deeper divide between conservative and liberal-minded parties that remains with us today."

Slightly impatient, while not showing it, the Reverend asked, "So, are you saying that racism in this country has grown in part because the number of foreigners arriving through immigration has increased?"

She nodded while sipping her tea before saying, "Yes. Actually it's been fairly dramatic in recent years, though still nothing like France or Canada. When Britain joined the European Economic Community in 1973, the level of migration from Western European nations increased. Migration from newer EU member states in Central and Eastern Europe since 2004 has resulted in a growing Eastern European presence in the UK. Back in 1950, there were only 20,000 non-white residents in the UK, most of them living in or around London. "

Again, Spelling seemed slightly perturbed by all the mathematical figures. Realizing it, Nanayakkara summarized. "Basically, the majority of people in England reside in the southeast, right where St. Anne's is situated. But that dense a population is inevitably being transformed by immigration. And, with Brexit, no one knows how much of the European population with make the trip to the UK, or vice versa. We are not as white as we were, and that change is occurring rapidly."

Nanayakkara stopped then, leaving her companions lost in their thoughts.

"So, what are our key considerations then?" asked Scarlett. "Clearly, if we seek to diversify the work of St. Anne's in a manner that reflects the changes in the country, there will be implications with language, cultural norms, even more food diversity for this kitchen," she concluded, gesturing to the room they were in.

"And religion," Nanayakkara added. "As people near death, faith takes on an immediacy that will have an impact at this hospice."

The Reverend seemed suddenly alert. "Of course, of course," he interjected. "That makes sense. But it means that the Judeo-Christian practices so well ensconced in this structure must give way to deep beliefs of Buddhism, Hinduism, Islam, etc. Death is common to all, but the faith one requires at the end is far broader than the Christian persuasion."

Scarlett, understanding the implications, grasped Nanayakkara's hand in hers. "You have provided us with what could be our greatest challenge as an organization. And you're right to wonder if we actually have the capacity to undertake such a transition. Perhaps we need to reconsider this step, given all the challenges before us."

This was unexpected, and placed a certain dulling effect on what had been the excitement of the board meeting. Everyone understood that the world was changing. But hospices had lived in something of an isolated state within their communities. That meant change might have come later to them than other organizations or institutions dealing with large segments of society – change that required updated policies reflecting the new realities.

"One of the wonderful things about religious faith, regardless of the religious persuasion, is that it teaches us that any sacrifice undertaken usually leads to transformational results. We see that in this place every day, as the dynamic and depth of the human heart and mind rise to inevitable challenges with a spirit that always surprises us. Yes, the various ethnic constituencies will be a greater challenge, but there will also be new varieties of compassion, faith, even giving that we must never forget. Should we go down this road at St. Anne's, it's not just about the sacrifices we will have to make but the benefits of us creating a space of larger human understanding and empathy."

Scarlett thought about these final sentiments of Reverend Speller as she journeyed back to Mulladore. He was the oldest of them all and likely threatened most by all these changes. But he also had the experience of years of living. From these he knew that divine humanity can never be measured in a moment but in a process, one that builds upon its strengths over years, and even centuries. Both she and Nanayakkara had smiled at one another at the end of his words, quietly agreeing that his age had actually expanded his understanding, not limited it.

These reflections dissipated gradually the closer she got to Bert's door. The darkness was beginning to envelop the horizon, and he would usually have his porch light on by now. Instead, the front threshold was giving way to the encroaching night.

Knocking on the door and receiving no response, Scarlett walked around to the side of the home and peered in a window. Bert was there, seated in his favourite armchair, asleep, with a book laying against his chest. The television was on, but he had clearly lost interest. She felt a heaviness somewhere inside her. This time of evening, her friend was usually working about the kitchen or carrying on some correspondence on his computer.

Quietly, Scarlett entered the rear door, which Bert usually left open, took off her shoes and shuffled into the room where he was still nodding off. There was a chill in the air and it prompted her to turn on the gas fireplace. She went through the house, turning off a couple of lights and making sure nothing was left on in the kitchen. Then she grabbed a comforter from the sofa, gently lifted the book from his chest, and laid the heavy fabric over him, up to his neck. Bert stirred momentarily but was gone again in an instant.

She felt badly leaving him in that position for the night, but sensed she should not disturb him.

A moment later, she was in Mulladore. Pouring a glass of red wine, Scarlett placed herself in front of her own fire and stretched out. It was happening; her practiced eye always knew when a body was in its final decline. His physical appearance hadn't changed appreciably, but it was clear that his energies were abandoning him. Fortunately, his mind was still as alert and attentive to his faculties as ever, so there was that. But Scarlett knew she was slowly losing the one person she had become closest to since first arriving at St. Anne's. That awareness briefly brought tears to her eyes.

Scarlett knew the time had come when she had to prompt a serious talk with her neighbour about his imminent future. Far from filling her with dread, she welcomed the chance to perhaps bring comfort into his troubled life.

And, as with her neighbour across the road, she nodded off in her most comfortable chair, the fire giving off the required heat, and her mind needing rest.

21

A gentle rap on the heavy wooden front door aroused Scarlett from what had been a dreamless sleep – rare for her. Swinging it open, she genially smiled at the sight of Bert. He was sporting an old fisherman's hat, and carrying a laminated tray with two plates full of potatoes, bacon, scrambled eggs, and salt and pepper, along with some dried toast with marmalade on the side.

"I just realized that none of this will go down very well without some coffee, which I trust you can brew up quickly." *He looks like his old self,* she thought, delighted at the sudden realization.

She quickly brewed two cups in the drip machine and placed their coffees beside the plates he had arranged. "I woke up this morning and noticed the fire going, the lights all out, and that I was covered with my mother's old comforter. And I realized only one person I knew would be so kind to arrange all of that. Thank you," he said, clinking his cup against hers.

It was one of the most pleasurable times with Bert that

she could recall. It was Sunday morning – one of those early spring moments when the sun shone brilliantly, somehow escaping the inevitably slanting rainstorms that came at the end of winter. Acknowledging this rarity, she rose and opened the casement kitchen window situated on the leeside of Mulladore, away from the chill of the morning breeze.

"Did you see your specialist this past week?" she asked, thinking it better to jump right into what surely was the most vital subject of the moment.

"Yes, and there's nothing new or urgent. His team inquired if I would be willing to permit an exploratory biopsy. When I asked if they could do anything about whatever they discovered, there was merely a shaking of the heads. My path is set. Now my task is to prepare the way."

Her eyes moistened as she reached over, placing her hand on his forearm - the sinews of strength from his carpentry labours still apparent, despite his obvious weight loss. "That needn't be a path meant for you to take alone," she uttered. "I would like to walk it with you."

Bert's averting gaze told her that he was moved by her words. This was the moment she had been waiting for and she felt the mood, the atmosphere, and the sunshine made it perfect timing. It was a testament to their relationship that they could speak so openly with each other in ways that were neither overly critical or judgmental. If that weren't so, what she was about to introduce would have proved impossible.

"Did the specialist provide you a prognosis?"

"About the tumour, you mean?" he asked.

"No, the timing."

His eyes suddenly looked deep into her own, and she

knew in an instant that this would likely be the most intimate conversation they had known in their budding
friendship.

"Of course, they can't be sure," he began, "but usually
brain tumours take their time shutting down different parts
of the body prior to closing down everything altogether. In
my case, however, with the mass being in the very centre of
the brain, things will move faster, and the effects on my
body overall won't be as severe. It will be the brain that
closes down first."

Scarlett did her best to hold her gaze to his and not
show the turbulence of the emotions that she felt. "And the
time?" she asked again.

"As yes, how much time left? In their estimation, it
could be six months, maybe less."

Exactly as she thought. Her training and experience
had informed her on such things, given her a kind of sixth
sense regarding end of life. She couldn't have known it, but
that intuition arose from her knowledge of the soul – the
inner spirit – and not just the body. Scarlett captured the
look on his face as her friend accepted that his physical
frame was failing him, and she could sense the mild fear
that comes with not knowing what comes next.

"Bert, would you consider spending this next while at
St. Anne's? Especially after all you have done for the place,
it would be fitting."

He surprised her by turning his head quickly towards
the window over the sink, where the sun was occupying
itself bathing everything in its aura. She knew what he
would say before he said it.

"Thank you ... sincerely, Scarlett. But that would signal
that I'm at some portal that I'm not yet ready for. I did

wonder about it a short time ago, but my spirit is not yet ready to fade away. An observation by Nietzsche was in one of the books I read the other day: 'One should die proudly when it is no longer possible to live proudly.' I want to live proudly, you see, regardless of the short time I have left. I don't think it's my stubbornness or pride – at least I don't believe so. I think it must have something to do with inner dignity. Both of my parents possessed it and I suppose I do as well, though I didn't really see it until now."

They were quiet for a time, but it was a silence of great and heroic eloquence – the kind that end of life can induce in those open to it.

"What about family, Bert … or close friends? Don't you want them around right now?" she asked.

"We went over this before, Scarlett. Any family that I have left are distant cousins who I haven't seen for years and years. And friends? Well, yes there are some, but they are mostly from the architectural profession. I haven't seen them much in recent years, and with this pandemic, our professional association hasn't met since it started."

He looked up at her with an expression on his face that bemused her. "That leaves you as my abiding friend, I suppose," he said, grinning. "And it just so happens that I couldn't have chosen a better companion for this last part of my journey. I mean, you're a hospice director. How fortunate is that?"

It was meant to be humorous, but she didn't take it in that spirit. "Bert, I want to be there as your friend, not as a professional. You have become my great neighbour, and I just want to be … well, *here.*"

Silence again, broken by his simple question: "Do you recall those early discussions we had shortly after you

arrived, when I told you that I preferred to live my life in isolation, without the burden of having others in my life? I knew you didn't take to that, but it has been my choice, and I believe in it now. There were times when I thought of marriage and children, but I saw what had happened to many of my associates, how they lived in marriages no longer loving and with children who had moved far away from home. I just didn't want that encumbrance in my life. And now that it nears its end, I'm glad in a way, since I don't have to worry about the fate of others when I'm gone.
"

"But, it's not over yet – your journey, I mean," she countered. "You might not feel as secure in your solitariness as you do now, Bert. There might come a time when you require another person, a kindred spirit, to take those final steps with you."

"That's what you're here for," he blurted in a kind of forced laughter that she understood immediately was prompted by his heavy medication. He caught it, too, and reddened in embarrassment.

"And I will be there, Bert – always – but I think you view the hospice as the place where things end, whereas it's really the threshold to what comes next. It's a launching pad for the spirit to continue on its next part of the journey."

"*A launching pad?* An interesting choice of words, Scarlett."

"Yes, probably not the best. But you catch my meaning, Bert, I know you do. It's the point of embarkation to whatever comes next. Do you not believe that?"

"Living in England for my entire life, I have been churched enough to have it engrained into my semiconsciousness. But to be honest, I have been too busy or distracted to give the idea of immortality any serious thought. It would probably be right to admit that I've purposefully avoided those things in life that make one too dependent on others – all this in my own quest to become unbreakable."

"Become unbreakable?" she half-blurted. "Bert, is something like that even possible? And why would someone desire that? I mean, they wouldn't be human, would they?"

"Oh Scarlett, that's four questions in rapid succession you've just asked, and I think I'm a little too tired right now to answer them properly. I think it's time for me to head back. Thanks for the coffee, and I'll leave the leftover food with you. I doubt you get much time for meal preparation these days. Perhaps I'll see you this afternoon."

She watched him working his way across the road and into his house, thinking repeatedly that she had overdone it over breakfast. He had looked like his old self when he first arrived, but her mini-inquisition had sapped his vigour, and she berated herself for her excess. Nevertheless, the subject of Bert and the hospice had been broached, and she had to content herself with that as she began clearing up the remnants of their morning meal together.

22

Later that same afternoon, as the early spring sun began its rapid descent into the west, Scarlett journeyed out into the large garden that encompassed Mulladore on all four sides. Ravages of the winter lay everywhere – fallen branches, and remnants of ungathered leaves, which she knew would eventually provide countryside habitats for summer's butter-flies, foxes, toads, shrews, earthworms, even the rare Siberian chipmunks that so captivated naturalists of the region.

She busied herself collecting the downed branches and placing them in piles, occasionally looking across the road for any sign of Bert. She once spotted his head in the kitchen window, hoping he would emerge shortly after … but nothing.

Scarlett was about to head inside to prepare a light lunch when she noticed someone walking through the short-grass meadow situated between St. Anne's and Mulladore. Rev. Thomas Spelling's form was unmistakable. Very tall, thin, narrow of hip and possessed of a great head of silver-grey hair. As always, his clerical collar was nestled between his Adam's apple and the turned-down collar of his knee-length spring Burberry coat.

"Missed you at church this morning," he said good-naturedly from over the fence.

Scarlett wiped a batch of dirt from her cheek, effectively smudging it even further, and prompted an unrecognized grin from her visitor. "Sorry, Tom, I had a visitor for breakfast," she responded, head nodding in the direction of Bert's home.

"Ah, yes, and how is he doing, our man of miracles?"

"In process, is about all I can say," she said sadly. "He's been given about six months, perhaps less."

They moved into the kitchen to escape the chill. Rev. Spelling requested coffee instead of tea – all this while continuing to speak of Bert's condition.

"I'm a bit surprised to see you at this time on a Sunday," she said, changing the subject. "How was church?"

He stirred the offered cream into his mug and mused, "I'm old enough to remember how church services, especially for the Church of England type, were as regular as four o'clock tea and an afternoon stroll in the woods. Folks like that are now mostly gone, and the newer generations prefer anything but tea and prefer touring in their foreign-made cars. It's a change, for sure, and it's meant that churches are slowly emptying out, not only of people but of their history."

Just the way he uttered that last phrase created a sense of sadness to move through her emotions, like a passing shadow. She knew he was right. It was happening around the world. The Christian influence, with all its ills and enlightenment, was slowly moving off.

"Well, I'm sure you're not here to regurgitate your homily for me," she said in an effort to change the subject.

"Oh no, you wouldn't wish that," the cleric muttered through a subtle laugh. I've actually been unable to think of little else since our private discussion with Saanvi Nanayakkara in the kitchen following the board meeting. What did you think of it?"

Scarlett, too, had been slightly overwhelmed by Saanvi's insights. "Well, I'm not sure 'troubling' is the right word, Tom, but I found it all a bit disorienting."

"Yes, that describes my sentiments at the moment. Where do we go from there?"

Warming up their coffees, she considered what to say next. The man across the table from her had been Scarlett's main support since before she even arrived – resolute, loyal, understanding, and appreciably humble. She could see he was troubled, so she chose her words carefully.

"To be honest, until Saanvi explained the current UK demographic situation, I hadn't really considered the implications on St. Anne's – the entire hospice movement, actually. We can't deny what she put before us because the data is all right there. We just never considered the implications."

"Well, I certainly hadn't," he observed. "My entire life has been spent living within these shores, and while I certainly noticed the growing plurality of our population, I had always seen our hospice as a bastion against all the massive struggles and changes in the world."

"What Saanvi said was that if we proceed with the plans to diversify our operations, then we will become the focus of all that change and turbulence. St. Anne's will be transformed into being not just a place of solace, but of complexity."

Spelling considered her words, looked directly at her, and asked, "Are we ready for that, Scarlett? I mean, do we have the capacity to adapt to what's coming?"

A sigh was all that escaped her lips for the first while. She had thought about this very thing ever since the board meeting. "I don't think we do, Tom," she said at last. "Eventually, it will change every aspect of our operation, and I'm not sure that a pandemic season is the right time to make such moves."

He nodded in agreement. "Exactly. That's just as I see it. But how do we reverse course? What do we tell Saanvi and her newly formed committee? Whatever we say will look like we are shying away from reality, from this new Britain."

"I know. However, it's not really our decision, but the board's. They conceded to it, and we'll just have to ask them to walk it back for a bit."

"Walk it back? I don't understand." His eyes were upon her, pleading for insight.

"I just mean that I believe we should keep the committee moving forward, but that we should take our time, perhaps even years, to absorb the changes in the best way possible. We need to consider all the implications and then we will be required to prepare for them. And I think, given her deep understanding and personal experience, that Saanvi is just the person to guide us through all this exploration. She won't just look at things strategically; she'll go out and visit those diverse communities and get their leaders onside. She's good at that."

The Reverend visibly relaxed. He leaned back, creaking the back of his wooden chair in the process. "I thought you perhaps felt the same way I did. Part of my relief, I suppose, is that if it is a lengthy process, much of it will likely take place after I'm gone."

"Me, as well."

He looked up in undisguised alarm. "Is there something you're not telling me? The best thing I ever did for St. Anne's was leading the recruiting campaign to get you. You've done wonders and, in the changes ahead, we'll need your guidance more than ever."

"I have no plans for leaving, Tom, but this process is likely to take some time and we can't predict the future that far in advance."

Later, at the door, she gave him a hug, then watched him round the corner for his walk back through the countryside and to the church. Out of habit, she gazed across the road. With yet a few hours of daylight remaining, she spotted no activity at Bert's. Thinking of sauntering across, she thought better of it and opted for a late-afternoon nap. She loved her English Sundays, regardless of the season, but realized that her life was becoming more complicated, both personally and professionally. She wasn't able to sleep, her mind racing incessantly. So she moved into the kitchen to prepare a light dinner, as her thoughts were taken up with the important days ahead.

23

As spring moved into full bloom, welcome news came from thousands of sources around the world that the Covid-19 virus was slowly losing its momentum. Following months of being one of the worst infected regions on the planet, the UK took sterner measures that eventually began paying off, leaving England, Scotland, Wales, and Northern Ireland some wiggle room regarding opening up their respective societies and economies.

That proved more difficult for the health sectors, however. Long lines of citizens requiring surgical procedures, put on hold due to the virus, took up whatever slack might have been created. For St. Anne's, frequently shut down through different phases of the pandemic, getting back to a semblance of normality meant that life remained just as hectic, yet with more of the pacing of regular hospice life.

Following the heart-to-heart conversation at Mulladore between Rev. Tom Spelling and Scarlett, the hospice board opted to charge Saanvi Nanayakkara's new committee on

163

diversity to first take on a capacity study before any further consideration be given to expanding hospice services to a broader range of ethnic communities. That took the pressure off – a welcome relief for Scarlett, as she attempted to get St. Anne's back to a modicum of routine, while at the same time working the board's barrister and charter accountant to streamline the financial donations that continued to come in at an unprecedented pace.

On a Thursday morning, she received an unexpected visit from Reverend Spelling, who rapped gently but rhythmically on her door post to catch her attention. Scarlett looked up with that same friendly smile that always charmed him. "Well, this is a nice surprise," she exulted. "Come in. Sit down here," she said, pulling a chair in his direction. "Want tea, coffee, or anything?" she added.

"No, no. I'm fine, Scarlett, honestly."

A quality in his tone along with the subtle diverting of his eyes told her that something had happened. "Are you alright, Tom?" she asked, concern clearly implied in her words.

The cleric moved forward gingerly until he stood across from the other side of her desk. "I was just visiting an old parishioner at Buckland Hospital who suffered a heart attack last month. He's progressing well enough, but as I was leaving the hospital, I noted that Bert Wynman was in a wheelchair at the admissions desk. He didn't look well, and before I could get to him, they wheeled him down one of the corridors. I took the liberty, as a hospital chaplain, of inquiring as to his circumstances. They called in his doctor and she informed me that he had collapsed at a coffee shop in Whitfield and was rushed to Buckland. I filled her in on his brain cancer prognosis, which she thanked me for, since they were still trying to rustle up his medical file."

As Spelling relayed this information, Scarlett rose from her chair, rounded her desk, and stood close to him. Her eyes brimmed with tears as she listened to the news. When he was finished, Tom moved towards her, placing a hand on her shoulder. She moved past it quickly and into his arms, tears now fully flowing.

A short while later, they sat in the two easy chairs by the window, mostly in silence. "I know what you're thinking, you know?" he said softly. "You believe you should have been there for him more than you were."

She merely nodded, then said, "It's true. Things at St. Anne's have been so all-consuming that I haven't had any time for myself, let alone my neighbour. And I could see he was failing quickly. I should have been there, but I know that's a normal feeling in such situations. I just can't shake it."

"Well, let's do something about that feeling. If you have some time at lunch, why don't we go together to see Bert? With my clerical advantage, I can get us both in to see him. Just don't let your regrets get the best of you. Right now, he just needs his good friend to be as positive as she can."

Buckland Hospital was a union workhouse infirmary when it first opened in 1836. Subsequently, it underwent numerous alterations and became a county hospital in World War Two, joining the National Health Service following the end of the conflict. But it was clearly outdated. Funding for a new purpose-built modern hospital was approved on an adjacent site in 2012, and it was completed three years later.

The health complex was at peak capacity by the time

Bert Wynman arrived at admissions, was channeled through the emergency department, and portered to his room on the third floor. Private rooms were no longer available in the COVID era, and Bert shared his space with a former ferry worker who had worked the English Channel between Dover and Calais. He had been happily retired to his English country cottage when he suffered a heart attack.

Tom and Scarlett were both permitted to briefly visit Bert as he was getting settled in. He smiled wanly at the sight of them entering from the corridor, but they could see that it was genuine. Not even attempting to rise, he motioned for them to take the two chairs stored in the corner.

"Well, I wasn't expecting you quite so soon, but I'm happy you're here." His voice was reedy, and he appeared exhausted.

"I had some inside information," the Reverend replied through a grin.

"Yes, I suppose you would."

Scarlett touched his elbow and asked, "This came kind of suddenly, didn't it?"

He nodded while shutting his eyes. "I was at my favourite window table at the Pillar Box Cafe in Whitfield, reading the Guardian, when I suddenly realized I couldn't focus on the printing. The next thing I knew, a kind server was beside me, claiming I had passed out. When I tried to stand, I just slipped off the chair and ended up on the floor. She called an ambulance, and here I am."

"Well, I'm glad you're safe," Scarlett said.

"Thanks. At least we know what it is, so I don't have to

go through a series of new tests to determine the problem. It just came on a little sooner than I expected."

"It must have jolted you a bit," Tom observed.

"More like it disoriented me, really. I have been tired in recent weeks, but never felt faint before. It was a little embarrassing that the incident happened in public."

"Anything I … we … can do to help?" Scarlett asked amiably.

"Well, according to the doctor, my condition appears to be arriving at a serious enough stage that I might not be returning home for any length of time. I wonder if you wouldn't mind keeping watch over the house and making sure the flowerbeds don't get too overgrown with weeds."

He suddenly stopped, lost in thought. "Actually, it's a silly request, isn't it?" he continued. "I mean, I'll hardly be tending those beautiful plants anymore."

A heaviness settled over the room, driven by the realization that Bert's final weeks were actually here, no longer in the future. Practiced in such moments, Reverend Spelling moved slightly towards the bed while the frail man looked at him with bemusement.

"I know what you're going to say, Reverend, and I appreciate it because I have come to know you so well in recent weeks. It would be right to say that religion and I have kept a respectable distance from one another in these past years, but that wasn't because I rejected it outright. My life was just busy. The Church of England has run like a tributary through my family for generations, and I'm sure I will be turning my soul in that direction shortly. But not just now. I have just arrived here and haven't even had the luxury of being able to assess my situation … and my options. When the time comes for my soul to make its preparation, it's you I will reach out to, Tom."

Scarlett always marvelled at how her neighbour always seemed to have a handle on things by seeing them in context. He was at it again now, helping Tom to feel needed while fighting for his right to have some space in the meantime.

Reverend Spelling barely caught the look in Scarlett's eye, but understood it immediately: she wanted some quiet time with the patient.

"Look, I'm one of the on-call chaplains for Buckland and have a couple of other folks to see before we leave. I'll leave you two for a bit while I do my rounds." He moved forward and offered Bert his hand. "I am at your beck and call, my friend." And with that he was out the door.

"Well, that went a bit easier than I thought it would. I wasn't quite ready for my Last Rights yet, but he handled it perfectly. I can see why the two of you have helped to bring St. Anne's so far."

Scarlett merely sat there, her kind eyes roving his gentle face. Eventually, the silence prompted him to ask, "Something on your mind?"

"Yes, Bert," she began hesitantly. "This is a marvellous structure with a first-rate staff, but somehow it doesn't feel like the right place for you."

His responsive grin was kind. "That's because you have a certain bias, my dear," he said.

She pretended to punch his shoulder. "Yes, yes, of course I do, and I admit it openly."

"Scarlett, I am here to die. Who would have thought it when you first arrived, but my time has come in a rush. I just require a place to prepare myself for that moment. Surely you understand that."

"Of course, and it's natural. But not at a hospice, not at St. Anne's."

"What does that mean?"

"It means that you would be there to live until the appropriate time, not die. There is a profound difference. Seriously, Bert, the world is just a great hospice. People live and die and live and die, but are often distraught as the moment draws nearer. St. Anne's isn't like that, never has been. You'll never be some mere patient there, but the centre of a celebration of your remarkable life. It's folks like you that make St. Anne's special, not the rest of us. We will honour all that you have done, and we will rejoice with you that the next place on your destination will be even greater than here. Surely you should give us that chance."

The intensity in her words wasn't discomforting, but it did a remarkable job of focusing his mind. "Perhaps what you're saying is that you should have that chance."

She wanted to demur, but instead let out a sigh of relief at having said what she said. "Of course, that's what I'm saying. You are my friend and my neighbour. The scriptures say we should love our neighbours, and, in this case, that was easy. But loving you as a friend? That has been one of the great privileges of my life."

They stared at one another, for some reason out of words. Everything seemed different now that they were here. In his calculating fashion, Bert was already working out what came next, making it easier to have an open discussion.

He looked up at Scarlett with a visage she couldn't quite place. He suddenly seemed almost spiritual or soulful.

He affirmed that observation when he said, "I'll tell you what, Scarlett. I'll commit to being transferred to St. Anne's, not because of all the valid reasons you listed earlier, but because I will be nearer to you. If you were stationed here, I would remain, but you have been a good friend, a wonderful example of refined compassion, and you happen to have remarkable organization skills. You're a good person to be with, especially on the last leg of my journey."

She couldn't help herself, bursting fully into tears while burying her face in her hands. He reached out to place his hand on her shoulder, as the sun slowly lowered towards the horizon.

24

True to his word, Bert had himself transferred by ambulance to St. Anne's two days after Tom and Scarlett's visit. They waited by the entrance for his arrival. He was fit enough to walk from the vehicle and into the front lobby area. The fireplace gave off a comforting heat as he sat on one of the leather single sofas, with his two friends seated opposite.

This was customary, as a measure of getting the patient used to the attractive and intimate surroundings of the structure. Bert had been in a few times recently, but never in his present capacity – or incapacity. Scarlett could see he was putting on a brave face, but was nevertheless dealing with the truth faced by any person entering a hospice: this was to be his final stop.

They enjoyed some tea together, though the Reverend opted for his favourite coffee. The dismal rain outside could be seen carving its path down the large floor-to-ceiling windows across the southern perimeter of the lobby.

"What documents do you have for me to sign?" asked

Bert, showing a level of discomfort in his new surroundings.

"We can take care of that later, in your room," responded Scarlett. "I'm just glad you're here, Bert. When you're ready I can show you to where you'll be staying. Have you let any family members known you're here? If so, we can help accommodate them if they plan to visit St. Anne's."

"I've asked one of my cousins to phone the others and inform them. They have the address for here, but I'm not expecting anyone. We'll see."

Reverend Spelling felt a strange sadness come over him and almost said something. Scarlett intervened before he could utter anything, saying, "Don't worry about it, Tom, it's all part of what Bert calls becoming unbreakable."

"Wh ... what?"

"Don't worry, I'll tell you about it later."

Bert expressed his satisfaction with the room. It possessed old-fashioned bookshelves, windows with lattice-like steel, and what would have been a lovely view of the meadow beyond had the rain let up somewhat.

"I hope I didn't put anyone out here," Bert said softly. "The history in this room is wonderful."

"All the rooms have similar amenities, and I didn't pull any strings, if that's what you mean?"

"I'm thankful for that," was all he said.

Scarlett showed him the washroom and separate shower/bath combo, along with a side room containing a television and computer terminal. Following that, she took him for a tour of the main components of the structure, including a fairly vast library, small swimming pool, infirmary, kitchen, and dining room, and finally the beautiful chapel with vaulted stained glass windows.

"I often wondered about this room whenever I drove by," Bert said.

"What do you mean?"

"You'd have to have an architect's eye to catch my meaning, but the way the beams are angled and joined was a master piece of carpentry. You can see the two roofs joining at different angles from the outside, and now that I'm in here I can see the results. It's beautiful."

And it was. There was enough room to seat about sixty people. Anglican hymn books were scattered along the pews, and a small ornate organ made of stained oak with copper fittings sat off to the side. Directly at the front was a small altar, behind which was the largest of the windows, depicting Christ in a position of prayer.

"Look over here," Scarlett said, grabbing his elbow and turning the corner into a little room directly behind the organ. From floor to ceiling were deeply stained bookshelves, each covered over with a door of glass and oak trim.

"Oh my," was all he said.

"I know. I thought you'd like it. The books in these cases are centuries old, and many of them tell the stories of the great structures in the area, including train stations, cathedrals, grand estate homes, castles, and even this place. It's where I got that Witherby Publishing Group's *The Master Architecture of Fourteenth Century England* that I gave you a while back. Remember? It came from right here," she said, pointing to an empty slot beside two other copies of the same volume.

"I do remember," he replied. "In fact, I have it stored in my large suitcase for reading while I'm here."

Just then, her assistant, Delores, stuck her head in the doorway. "Sorry to disturb you – nice to see you, Mr. Wynman – but Scarlett, Reverend Tom wondered if you had a moment to speak with him in the kitchen?"

"Tell him I'll be right there." Scarlett moved towards Bert and gave him a gentle embrace. "Why don't you get settled in and we'll talk later about anything else you might require?" she said.

"I can't imagine anything – you've thought of it all," he said as a compliment.

"With an active mind like yours, I hardly think that's true," she replied. "I'll drop in later. You'll notice a little sign outside your door that you can use if you don't want to be disturbed."

She found Tom at one of the corner eating area tables, his mind clearly preoccupied. "I would say 'penny for your thoughts' normally, but by the look on your face, it could cost a fair bit more."

He looked up, motioned to the tea he had retrieved for her, and pulled her chair out. "I have something important to share with you, but before I do, it's important for you to know that I'm here on behalf of the board."

Spelling had been twirling a piece of foolscap between his two hands and now opened it to reveal a formal letter with a bright yellow sunflower at its top. Scarlett recognized it right away as the logo for Hospice UK.

"You should take this back to your office and read it in full, but it was addressed specifically to the board, so we are fully aware of its contents."

"Oh my, this sounds awfully serious," Scarlett

responded. "I see it's from Hospice UK, so it can't be that serious."

"Except that it is," he said immediately, clearly agitated. "It asks St. Anne's if we would be willing to support you if they asked you to take on the role of Director of the nationwide organization. They mentioned the way you have steered our organization through this crisis and the benefit you brought to the entire movement in your work with *Only Progress* and the BBC. " He took a quick sip of his coffee before adding, "It seems like they feel that the entire hospice movement could benefit from your marvellous skills."

And just like that, he was done. It was clear to her that it was all her friend dare say. Everyone would understand that it was her decision, and this letter only came by way of a courtesy to let the board know that Hospice UK would be about to make a direct appeal to her.

"Tom, I know the board would support this request, but how do they really feel about it?"

Another quick sip of coffee. "It would be fair to say that they are grieving somewhat – a fit response given the mandate of this place. We all realize that it was your efforts that took away any worries we might have had for our future. And it's not merely about economic security, you know? You have effectively reminded all of us what we are in this business for. You have raised the plight of those near end-of-life to national interest and in the process we have come to better understand our purpose at St. Anne's. I think that is what we will all miss the most." The last sentence was said almost in a whisper.

"Tom, this is all fully unexpected for me, but you seem to infer that I will be taking the offer."

"Well, why wouldn't you? It matches your skill level, and all of us as board members understand that it is the movement that matters most at present, especially in this pandemic. And we would have been honoured to have played a part in that, sad though it will be."

Half an hour later, she walked by Bert's room, but spotted the Do Not Disturb sign. *Just as well,* she thought. She had some serious thinking to do and, as it was nearing the end of the day, she chose to walk back to Mulladore to reflect on this new opportunity in her life and career. This wasn't going to be easy.

25

A heavy schedule, much of it related to the letter from Hospice UK, prevented Scarlett from visiting Bert until the following evening, by which time he had clearly acclimatized himself to his new surroundings.

The past day had been occupied with her meeting with representatives from the board. That was followed by an almost two hour video conference call with the executive of Hospice UK, and another call with one of the senior vice-presidents of the National Health Service who oversaw the hospice movement in the broader health delivery service of the nation. She could sense rather than see Rev. Tom Spelling walking the corridors of St. Anne's, knowing he would be fretting over the possible loss of his executive director and friend.

Scarlett was surprised at her lack of real interest in the choice she would soon have to make. Life had been so full of pathos and adventure that she had spent virtually no time on thoughts of her career. Why would she? Life near the southern coast of England had been nothing like what she had expected – she'd believed it would be a British version of her hospice experience in Nova Scotia. She hadn't counted on the unique position of St. Anne's, a pandemic, her relationship with her staff and patients, Sandy Templeton, the friendship with the Reverend, and, naturally, the unfolding relationship she and Bert had enjoyed in the past year.

The people on the screen facing her were complete professionals, aware of their responsibilities to the broader public and the health service itself. They had their facts well in hand: the aging population and the increased demand expected to be placed on hospices across the land as a result, the welcome climb in fundraising that followed the BBC special and the hopes it had provided for future revenue, the rapidly increasing movement towards extending services to "hospice at home" opportunities, and, inevitably, what would be expected of the new director.

She was interested to learn that the person she was being asked to replace had postponed her scheduled retirement until the COVID pressures had relaxed. That made her feel better, since she had wondered how the present director would feel about an upstart from Canada suddenly supplanting her in the role.

It became clear after a time, however, that what they were really seeking from her was the ability to fundraise – a surprise, since that had never been a real strength she considered herself possessing. Something about this desire for her abilities to bring in financial resources troubled her. Back in Nova Scotia, fundraising was just as serious, and she undertook it as part and parcel of her responsibilities as director. But it had never been her primary pursuit, nor did she have much of a liking for it.

Yet it was always nice to be appreciated. They offered generous benefits, and the home office for Hospice UK on Britannia Street in London looked open and airy, with windows everywhere. The ability to travel to the continent was also expected of the executive director, since much of the organization's connections were with European counterparts.

There was pressure from the recruiting committee for her to decide as soon as possible, owing to their desire to capitalize on the popularity she had recently achieved with the BBC. This made sense to her, but the demand was foreign to her nature. Nevertheless, the exchange with the home office was informative and appealing. She signed off the video conference finally taking it seriously that she had a decision to make – and soon.

From his breast pocket, Tom pulled out some paper covered with his familiar scrawl. "I did some research on Hospice UK and just how vast it is," he said as a means of starting the conversation.

She understood how difficult this was for him, and yet here he was, reminding her of the vast opportunity before her. "Anything you found interesting?" she asked.

"Well, Hospice UK and its network oversees the care of one-quarter of a million people a year who are in their final stage of life. But, in addition, last year they assisted 72,000 people with bereavement support, even after their loved ones passed away. That's pretty impressive."

"It is," she agreed, "but that's the way the entire hospice movement has been going in recent years – into private homes as opposed to hospice residences themselves. Health institutions are giving way more and more to self-care, mostly owing to the cost of institutional supports."

"It's interesting to hear you say that," he responded, "since Hospice UK reports that 83 per cent of its work is provided in community care settings, including hospice at home, out-patient hospice, even hospice day care."

She looked at him, clearly surprised. *"Eighty-three percent?* I had no idea."

"That's because St. Anne's never evolved in that fashion. We stayed with the old institutional model of people coming into one place. I must admit it surprises me too."

This was more than Scarlett bargained for. That same centralized model practiced at St. Anne's was how the hospice in Nova Scotia had worked as well. Clearly, the Brits had graduated more to this model of community care than some other jurisdictions.

"This has given me something to think about, Tom. Thank you for taking the time to research all that for me."

"No problem," he replied. "And there's one more item I think that you might find interesting. According to Hospice UK's annual budgetary report, the organization spent a total of £1.5 billion on their services in 2017-18, of which £969 million was spent on care, with £497 million spent on fundraising activities."

She looked up, surprised again. "In other words, a third of the funds they accrued in a single year went towards fundraising ventures?"

Tom merely nodded. After a moment, in which she silently remained in thought, he said, "It appears from this that a good half of your efforts will be spent on getting resources."

"Fundraising, you mean?" she replied. He nodded again.

"Just one more thing I thought you should know. There are at least 125,000 volunteers supporting hospices throughout the UK. The value of their contribution is estimated to be more than £200 million each year. You will actually be directing a small army."

"If I take the position," she countered.

"Yes, if you accept."

Scarlett broke off the subject and looked directly at her friend. "This is hard on you, I know, Tom," she said, almost in an outright apology.

The Reverend pretended to gaze out the window behind her, but was really carefully calculating what his next words would be.

"Yes, of course – hard on all of us, really. In truth, this structure has gone through little change. But the operation – the people, the profile, the connection to community, the staff – looks nothing like it did prior to your arrival. You seem to have the Midas touch when it comes to putting new wine into old vessels. It's a gift, and we know it. We also understand that we likely won't find the likes of it again."

He was right, she knew. Her success in this place had surprised even her. For whatever reason, this particular setting permitted her to come into her own as a leader – something that had been left largely unrealized back in Canada. But here, in this marvellous portion of southern England, the mixture had proved just right for the blossoming of her efforts.

"Tom, let me think about it, okay? I've always wanted to serve humanity, just like my parents, so the prospect of reaching millions more through the national organization is a profound opportunity to someone with that mindset. I haven't had time to develop any kind of leaning yet, but I vow to work with you through this entire process. Whatever the outcome might be, it will not happen in solitude, but with the collaboration of all of the people here – and especially you."

26

At last she made her way to Bert's room, quietly chiding herself for the delay and sensing a measure of hesitancy at whether her absence had been felt.

The first sight of him dispelled all concerns. The door, with his name card slid into the slot, was open, and she saw him inside, seated on the comfortable reclining easy chair, glasses on and concentrating fully on the pages of a book.

"Well, I'm happy to see you," he began immediately. But when he attempted to rise to greet her, Bert swayed, almost losing his balance. She moved to him quickly and helped him to recline again. She took the seat opposite and merely smiled at him.

"I've missed you, and I'm sorry it's been so busy. Can I get you a tea or coffee?"

"I've been prepared for you coming and have something special," he replied, reaching over the side of his chair and pulling out a bottle of French Sauvignon Blanc. He smiled directly at her. Scarlett looked at the clock on the wall and, seeing that it was the end of the workday, nodded with a grin.

"I'll get the glasses, while you open the bottle," she said.

While hunting for the appropriate long-stemmed glasses, she took a quick appraising look around Bert's suite and saw it was immaculate. In his practiced fashion, he had appointed it perfectly, with his favourite books on various shelves, and paintings or planned drawings of famous structures on the walls. In the background, she discerned the gentle tones of a female voice singing some tunes from years ago.

"It's Vera Lynn and her most famous songs from the war years," he said, as if discerning her thoughts. Everyone in the UK knew of Lynn, who had died recently at the age of 103.

"Funny," she said, turning around and carrying the glasses, "I didn't think you were that old."

Bert laughed. "There are a couple of reasons why I often listen to her. She was greatly loved by my parents, who were able to endure the Second World War, in part, because of the inspiration her singing brought them, and the nation."

"And the second?"

"Her most famous song was the 'White Cliffs of Dover,' which, for obvious reasons, makes me sentimental, since I spent my childhood there."

The music played uninterrupted in the background as he attempted to pour the wine with both hands. After some spilled on the wooden table between them, Scarlett reached out gingerly and assisted with the task. He was slightly embarrassed, she could tell, yet his genial nature easily overcame the difficulty of the moment.

Once the wine glasses were filled, they clinked them together before leaning back in their chairs.

She was about to ask about his condition when he observed, "I must admit, I didn't realize your life was this hectic here. I've walked around the hallways or been in the dining room but haven't spotted you at all."

"Well, that would be because I'm struggling over an important decision and have been preoccupied speaking with folks about it."

Scarlett laid out the invitation from Hospice UK for Bert and the implications for St. Anne's. She spared nothing and spoke openly of her ongoing state of indecision. He merely sat there, revealing nothing, as she came to the end of describing her difficulty.

"Well, that is one remarkable opportunity, especially for a woman from Nova Scotia," he said, smiling broadly.

"That's absolutely true, Bert. I didn't even know if I'd fit in when I first arrived here, and now I'm being asked to take a national post. It's just confusing."

"That's because it's not really about which position would be best for you."

She sat up immediately, thankful for his engagement in the subject. "What do you mean?" she prompted.

For whatever reason, Bert seemed absolutely prepared for what he was about to unfold; she could see it in his demeanour. What she was to hear in the next hour was about to refine her path in life and how she discerned herself.

"From my first meeting with you that day when I introduced myself, I thought you one of the oddest people I had ever met."

She burst into laughter, neither offended or embarrassed at the observation – merely intrigued. "We can talk about that later. Just keep going," Scarlett urged.

"Perhaps it's because you're from another culture, similar to ours but not the same. Or maybe living close to the sea in Nova Scotia, as I have here in England, has left you with a rhythmical view of humanity that doesn't subscribe to the endless progressive bent of modern life. Whatever it is, your view of life's path is both intuitive and evocative. I especially sensed it when you returned from Sicily and offered your view of death as a servant instead of a master. I walked home across the road highly intrigued."

Scarlett looked up in revelation. Her neighbour had never spoken like this before, nor had she discerned how he perceived her. "Bert, I never knew this."

"That's because you've been so busy helping others that you've overlooked your uniqueness in this place."

"Perhaps, but I think I began to sense it once the BBC got involved and everything seemed to change," she observed.

He looked at her impatiently. "That's not what I mean. This isn't about your ability to promote or raise funds for the hospice movement, which is what I suspect Hospice UK really desires from you. We're really speaking about who you are, despite all of that. I have frequently thought of you as someone trapped between science and philosophy, and being in the hospice movement accentuates it. In many ways you're a medical professional, well-trained and knowledgeable, and in that sense you are a credit to the medical community. But St. Anne's is more than that, isn't it? – or hospices in general, when you think about it."

"I'm not quite catching your meaning, Bert," she interrupted, slightly confused but highly intrigued.

"When you think about it," he continued, "modern healthcare is really a scientific process – a remarkable one, I'll give you that – but it seeks to isolate the patient in order to induce recovery and research. But hospices are about bringing a holistic world to the patient – family, friends, religion, culture – since the outcome is not in doubt. The health system accommodates such influences, as needed, but they are ancillary to the real pursuit of healing the body. Hospices don't accommodate but incorporate such things in the healing and preparing of the human spirit. The entire process would be impossible without those added elements."

He stopped for a minute and she knew better than to interrupt. This was good stuff – as was the wine, which they were both enjoying.

"It's no secret to anyone that much of what we enjoy in this world lies beyond answers and easy information. We aren't confronted with this reality so much anymore because of modern information technology. It brings the world to us, but doesn't really help us see our place within it. There is little that is 'unknown' anymore, since everyone loves the newest invention, which quickly becomes disposable as we move to the next great thing. All of this leaves little place for those great things that lie beyond us, and we lose our curiosity for them.

"This is where you come in, I think, Scarlett. You are effectively inspired and mobilized by that world that so many have forgotten. The problem for you is that you are a part of the scientific health collaborative, but your motivations don't come from there. That's what makes you such a wonderful maven for a hospice: you draw power from the human spirit itself, not all the things it invents."

She refilled their glasses and observed, "I have often thought that knowledge today is merely the adding of one bit of information on top of an older one, and, in the process, we have lost our sense of wonder at what we don't know because we think we have all the information we need. It's true what you're saying Bert. I just had never put myself in the middle of it."

Her friend leaned forward. "Well, you must begin to do that now, Scarlett, because the rest of your life will depend on it." As if struck by an inspiration, he added, "Do you know what I was reading as you came in? It was John Donne's observation of how the new world of science and discovery was in the process of displacing the awe and wonder passed on to us by our ancestors. Listen to this." He picked up the slim volume and began to read:

> *And new philosophy calls all in doubt,*
> *The element of fire is quite put out;*
> *Tis all in pieces, all coherence gone;*
> *All just supply, and all Relation ...*
> *And in these Constellations then arise*
> *New stars, and old does vanish from our eyes.*

"He penned that in 1611, just as science and new technologies were finding their way into the human story. He was a healthy mind, caught between science and intuitive knowledge. And that is where you are, my friend: caught between professional science and intuitive knowledge. What the ancients gave us still matters. Why do people continue to go against their best instincts? Where is God? Is there a God? How does one forgive? How do we keep tribalism from making us prejudicial towards others? How does one die well? How does one live well?

"None of these questions has been answered, despite all the recent centuries of scientific knowledge and acumen. And that is because such things are only understood through human experience: intuitiveness. Some things live beyond facts, and it is in those dimensions that the human soul must journey if it is to grow. We see the unknown as something which can be conquered as opposed to something which is beyond us and therefore minimizes our grand view of ourselves."

A great silence ensued. In Bert's mind, he had spoken too much, waxed too philosophical. But for Scarlett, he hadn't done nearly enough. She was becoming alive to the possibilities of what he was implying.

Just then, one of the volunteers entered the room, carrying two paper bags with labelling that revealed they were filled with Chinese food. "Oh dear, I forgot all about this," Scarlett said in mild alarm. "I took the initiative to order us dinner, and it promptly left my mind. Let me get the dishes."

And so, for a few moments at least, the vital narrative Bert had been weaving was left behind in favour of chicken fried race, chow mein, dumplings, won ton soup, and the inevitable fortune cookies. They were surprised at how hungry they both were.

"Do you have a sense of what I should do … about the Hospice UK offer, I mean?"

Bert was thoughtful for a moment, running things through his active mind. "I suppose that depends on whether you feel your work here is finished," he answered finally.

Scarlett had thought of this repeatedly over the last twenty-four hours and knew the answer. "I hardly think so. In fact, in some ways it feels like it's only beginning."

"You're different, Scarlett, you really are. You continually introduce people to other possibilities that have little to do with finality. With some things there is no progress, no completion, but only those invisible guideposts that we can't shape but which help us to understand ourselves. They provide humanity with the wonderful comfort of knowing that there are things greater than one's self, greater than the here and now. We can swim in the realm of the ocean of the unknown, where there is no shore and no bottom, only expanse and the need to keep moving. There is no map, only the journey. There is no end, only the unexpected."

Despite herself, Scarlett burst into tears – not of sadness but the joy of discovery. What her friend had just revealed, in all its eloquence, was who she was but had never been able to define. It was as if she was seeing herself in the mirror for the very first time, and she very much liked what she saw.

"Do you believe such things?" she asked, wiping the tears away.

"For you, I do. And I'm coming to realize that they have become vital to me. I suppose that awareness began when you returned home from your visit to your grandfather's grave at the Commonwealth war cemetery. Do you remember what you discovered at the bottom of his tombstone – the words, I mean?"

"All is not finished," she said, almost whispering in realization of where Bert was going with this.

"Yes. I found myself profoundly moved by those words,

and the possibility that life is not a beginning and an end, but a journey through many ends, many stages, each surpassed by something greater. This is why you are so necessary to the hospice movement, and most likely to St. Anne's. Those about to pass to the next stage from St. Anne's are living in a world of images and thought that transcends the world of everyday reality. If we are to understand them in such moments, we must listen, and we must create conditions where they can communicate those truths to us. Hospital care is about ministering to those people as they pass; hospice care is about them ministering to us, as we live. It's different, and it's beautiful, and it's far more vital than a world of starts and stops. They, in fact, are bringing life to us."

Bert picked up his fortune cookie, crunched it, and pulled out the small slip of paper from within. He looked at his friend. "I believe you live in between these two worlds, Scarlett, and are equally conversant in both. St. Anne's has opened your eyes to who you truly are, just as you have opened theirs to their potential. It's not about money, or leadership, or science, or even death. It's about the ongoing movement between those two worlds and your ability to navigate those waters. And it's my sense that you are still exploring that possibility here."

She wanted to move over, to embrace him, to acknowledge that, through his insights, she had discovered her depth. Then she spotted the sly grin of humour on his face.

"What's so funny?" she asked.

"Here's my fortune" he began, reading from the paper.

You will enjoy a long and prosperous life.

The irony of the moment came over them both and, outside in the corridor, others could hear the laughter ringing out like the bells of a church calling the faithful for worship.

For the first time in a week, Scarlett slept the entire night with no disturbance. The talk with Bert had cleared her mind of the hundreds of pieces of information retained from all the discussions regarding Hospice UK and the choices before her. It still being early, she sent a message to the chair of the hospice board, asking for a video conference for the board later that day, as she had some important details to discuss. She had no doubt that all members would be present.

As she set about cleaning the kitchen she had neglected for days, she looked out past the path to the road and at Bert's home. The realization hit her that she hadn't even thought of all the arrangements he would have to undertake to settle his estate. Scarlett had no idea what he had in the way of wealth, or even if his house was fully paid for. His classic Triumph Herald was still in the driveway, covered over with a tarp that he used to keep away the ravages of winter and the turbulent early spring.

It was likely he would never see his home again, nor did

he show any resolve to return. His rational mind would have told him that he was at his final station of life, and it was clear from her visiting his room at St. Anne's that he had sorted everything out to his liking. Still, she felt a tender sadness at the thought that his place of so many years would no longer feel the effects of his living and affectionate care. She made a mental note to bring up the subject of his estate when at the hospice later in the day.

The board had assembled online at the end of the day, dispensed with the usual regularities, and turned the meeting over to Scarlett. In the top left corner of her screen, she could see Reverend Speller looking out at her. He, more than anyone else, would want to hear what she was about to say.

It took her only five minutes to tell them that she had decided to turn down the offer from Hospice UK, and her ultimate reason was that she felt much was left to be done at St. Anne's. She was determined to take on that challenge with just as much energy and verve as she had demonstrated when she first arrived.

The relief was palpable. Some were exultant at the news, while others remained silent but smiling at the prospect. Their largest crisis was over, even greater than the pandemic itself. Without her influence, they likely would have been making huge sacrifices to their operation by now. But, as it was, they were now ready for whatever came next.

And this is where Tom took the discussion in the next moment. He expressed his deep appreciation for the decision that she had come to, and promised the board's ongoing support for whatever came next.

"For us to be behind you as much as we can, as the official board of St. Anne's, it would be helpful to know what you meant when you said, 'there is much left to be done.' What are you thinking?"

She looked at the computer screen before her, thankful for each person displayed there. Strangely, Scarlett felt little emotion. Instead there was a sense of resolve, and she was eager to get on with it. Looking at the person at the top left of the screen, she laid out her plan.

"As you know, we have decided, as a board, to do a deep dive into the issues of inclusiveness and diversity under the able direction of Saanvi. I think we've all realized how complex of an undertaking that will be – it will likely take years. However, I learned only yesterday that the vast majority of hospices in this country do more of their work out in the community than in the hospice structures themselves. I don't mind saying that it was a revelation to me, leaving me to wonder if it is time for St. Anne's to take its wonderful history, people, and care farther afield."

She smiled for a moment. "And here I was thinking that my place might be within the larger movement across the country, when all along I was missing the reality that this place has so much more to offer to the communities that already know us, resource us, and trust us. I find myself wondering if you'd be willing to take that journey with me. You know the region much better than I. But I can't help thinking that our place, our unique presence, belongs just as much out there, with them, as it does in waiting for them to come here at the appropriate time. This is a hospice movement, and that implies action on our part.

"I would like us to consider ways in which we might become more mobile, and I suspect that in doing so we will encounter those various communities of diversity that we have been talking about. To get them to come here is a tall order, for that is not their culture. But they are rich in the depths of the spiritual, the communal, and the rites of passage. I would like to meet them where they are at because anything so good as we have here can only be best expressed and lived out among the people, as diverse as they are."

There was silence, as most weren't sure if she was finished. But Scarlett had said it all, and that left the next step to the board itself.

Tom Spelling chimed in immediately with his approval, thanking Scarlett once again for not only remaining with them but having the tenacity to move forward rather than sitting on her laurels or past victories. Others voiced the same resolve, with the board chair asking if Scarlett would like it put to a vote. She demurred, saying that that time would come when the plans were put in place, along with the empowering budgets to enact the new vision.

Scarlett had just signed off on the call when a knock came at her office door. It was Delores, her special assistant. "I'm sorry to be the bearer of bad news, but Bert Wynman has just suffered a stroke. He's barely hanging on."

She was out the door before Delores finished, placing a hand on her shoulder before running down the corridor.

St. Anne's contained a medical procedure room for sudden emergencies, but the doctor had chosen to leave Bert in his own room, in his own bed. Scarlett entered swiftly but gently and took a place beside Dr. Amahle, a female doctor from South Africa.

"I'm sorry, Scarlett, I know this is difficult, but we expected something like this soon enough. Mr. Wynman's brain was attempting to keep so many things going at the same time. It was inevitable it would become overloaded, especially with the cancerous tumour in its centre."

"Can he understand us, or hear us?" Scarlett asked.

"No, those senses aren't functioning; the stroke appears total," Amahle responded. "He is stable for now, but he won't have long. Why don't I continue my rounds and come back later. Again, Scarlett, I'm so sorry." With that, she was out the door, leaving the two friends alone in the same room where they had shared Chinese food only the evening before.

Bert's eyes opened and closed intermittently. But when Scarlett stood directly in his line of sight, they remained open, attempting to focus. She quickly scanned the checklist at the end of the bed, noticing that Bert hadn't requested a cleric at the time of passing. Nevertheless, she brought out her cellphone and texted Reverend Tom to come to the room a.s.a.p.

She naturally grabbed Bert's hand and cradled it in both of her own. "Oh, Bert, my friend, I'm sorry we didn't get more time. I know you can't hear me, but I just need to say that you have turned my professional life on its head and my personal life into a great adventure. I can never thank you enough."

Looking into his eyes, she thought she detected recognition in them. They warmed imperceptibly, but enough to give her a sense of connection. Pulling a chair close by, she got down to his level and brought her face closer to his. "Bert, you said yesterday that death is but a step into the next stage of life. And you said that I had an intuition about such things. Well, I'm having one of those intuitions right now. You and I are not done. There is more to come for both of us, but right now especially for you. Believe in that, if you can, Bert. The next stage in our incredible existence is but one step away. Take it in stride, and use that brilliant mind of yours in whatever comes next. You are dear to me, so dear."

To her surprise, his eyes narrowed on her, and she could see his lips attempting to move. She came closer to them, holding her ear down to listen. When the whispered words came, they brought one of the greatest assurances she had ever known.

"All is not finished," he uttered through a whisper. Tears cascaded down her cheeks and she sobbed openly. Scarlett looked into his eyes again, as deeply as possible, and was about to say, "I know. I know," when she suddenly realized the light had gone out of them. He was gone, the light in those eyes now illuminating the place where he now was.

Just then, Tom rushed into the room and his practiced eye discerned in a moment that he was a fraction too late. "He's gone?" he asked.

She rose and moved immediately into his arms. "No, he's just moved off into his next great adventure." Then she wept at not being able to share it with him – not yet.

EPILOGUE
MULLADORE

Bert's funeral was held on a Friday morning – a traditional and dignified Church of England service. Tom Spelling led the service, giving a moving homily, at the end, on the power of the individual life, peppered with architectural analogies and Bert's love of learning.

Scarlett was surprised how few attended. There were relatives, not many, and a few of his associates from the architectural society. There were actually more present from the hospice community than from his own personal life. Upset at first, she eventually came to terms with the understanding that this was as her friend would have wanted it. Still, it was difficult.

Spring now in full bloom, the committal was held outside in the church cemetery, the bright sun eventually overcoming the chill of the day. The headstone wasn't in place – delayed like much else, due to the pandemic. Bert's coffin was made of his favourite oak, with brass handles and a natural finish.

She stayed at the gravesite as the others all departed to

carry on with the rest of their day. Tom had wished them God's speed and returned to stand beside Scarlett, his stately robe flowing out, at times, in the wind.

"We haven't had much of a chance to talk, with all that's going on," he observed. "Grief is a funny thing. Some wish to talk going through it, while others prefer living within their own thoughts. I wasn't sure which of those you were and decided not to call, out of respect, of course."

"You made the right choice, Tom. I'm one of the latter."

"I meant what I said in the message, you know. When you think about it, Bert's influence was fundamental to where we are now. The awareness, the resources pouring in, the more secure future – he quietly brought all that about. But his main accomplishment, I think, is how he transformed my dear friend Scarlett. I think those final days with him affected you more than most of us, perhaps any of us, imagined."

Scarlett began putting on her gloves as she said, "It was the final talk we had on that last night before he passed. He had me figured out perfectly. I'm in this place, hovering between being a health professional and something of a mystic. I had never understood that duality before in such terms, but he was right. I knew in an instant that my place was here, helping St. Anne's to extend its quality and privileges to the larger community. He passed away before I could ever thank him fully for that gift.

They hugged goodbye, and she began her walk back to the hospice. As she arrived, Charlotte, the receptionist, pointed to a man seated in the corner. "He's asking for you, Scarlett. What should I do?"

"Did he say who he was?"

"Mr. Wynman's solicitor, I believe he said."

Scarlett smiled at her and moved over to the guest. His facial features were somewhat difficult to make out because of the COVID mask he was wearing, but she could see he was of medium height, with graying hair, and carrying a satchel.

"Hello," she said to him, prompting him to rise and give a short nod.

"Ms. Scarlett Carlyle?" he asked.

"Indeed."

"I'm Sinclair Arnold, Bert Wynman's solicitor in charge of his estate. Is there somewhere we can talk in private?"

"Certainly. How about my office? Have you had lunch?"

"No, afraid not," he replied.

She offered a pleasant smile. "Well, the kitchen is offering vegetable soup and salmon sandwiches. How does that sound?"

"Wonderful … thank you kindly."

They sat across from one another, the inlaid wooden coffee table between them. Lunch would be delivered shortly.

"How can I help you, Mr. Arnold?" she asked, deeply curious as to the visit.

"I'm here as a representative of Mr. Wynman's estate. He left a will and asked that I carry it out once he was gone."

"Well, that would keep you busy, I suspect. He had a wide influence, especially in the architectural field."

"Yes, one would think. But that isn't the way that his will is structured." He paused a minute, considering his next words. "Perhaps the best thing is just to lay out for you what he desired. While he left some financial endowments to a few relatives and to the architectural society he served for so many years, he has left everything else to St. Anne's Hospice, including his house, land, and a generous financial sum."

"Oh, my … I had no idea. He never said anything about this to me. Was his decision recent?"

"No, it was about six months ago that he asked for my help in crafting the will. He was very firm in charging me that I do a thorough job of making sure that everything he left to the hospice be administered in full."

"Yes, that's just like him," she said with a smile.

"The reason I came to you, Ms. Carlyle, is due to your position as head of St. Anne's hospice. Normally, I would first approach your solicitor or chartered accountant, but it was Mr. Wynman's request that I deal with you directly. Apparently, the two of you are also neighbours."

"And friends," she replied.

Scarlett didn't bother to ask how much the entire endowment to St. Anne's would be, but she had no doubt it would be substantial. She offered to put Arnold in touch with the board chair so they could move on transferring the estate from there."

Later, over a quick lunch in which they discussed many of Bert's activities and successes, the solicitor reached into his satchel and produced a white envelope with her name inscribed on the front. "He asked that I give this to you directly," was all he said as he passed it over.

She felt as though she were about to touch an electrical current. This was unexpected, and everything within her wanted to open it then and there. Sensing this to be so, Arnold rose to his feet, saying he had to be going.

As they walked to the front door, she asked, "Do you know when he wrote this letter?"

"I think it was just a few days ago. I believe it was on his first day here."

Scarlett thanked him, saw him out to his car, and decided to walk the short distance to Mulladore to digest the letter there. She was nervous and exhilarated in the same moment.

She put the fire on, grabbed some iced tea, and sat on the sofa. Tearing it open as gently as she could, knowing that the contents would likely be something for posterity, she unfolded the three sheets of paper, and admired the precise handwriting. There was no date and she began reading:

Scarlett:

By this time, you will know that I have left a number of things to St. Anne's Hospice. One of the things that made that choice easy was knowing that you would know best how to distribute them in the ways you think most suitable. You'll protect the spirit in which I give them, I know.

Perhaps one of the most difficult things for you to decide is what to do with my home. So much of my attention has gone into it that little within it has been left untouched by my hands. Perhaps you might find it suitable as some kind of annex to St. Anne's or just to be used as some kind of investment property to help guard the longevity of the hospice in lean times. It's funny how we spend so much time on such things and then, in a moment, they are of no use to the owner. Perhaps my spirit can continue on in the uses to which it is put.

One of my great regrets, and there aren't that many, is that you and I didn't know one another earlier. Something about you, from that first moment we met, told me that this person was so unique as to be of great use to humanity. I also understood almost immediately that you would not leave my life unchallenged. I, who had been so careful to keep my guard up, was well enough aware that you would attempt to break it down – not because you are one of those nosy people, but because you were sharp enough to see the damage I was doing to myself by being so remote.

You were right, of course. To keep myself from being hurt or broken, I forgot to take into account that I had grown impervious to love and humanity. As my end approached, I came to understand too late that it is precisely those delicate things in us that open us up to the wonders of life.

Yes, I bemoan that we didn't meet one another earlier. But imagine if our connecting had come too late! I would have been a man, confined to a hospital and incapable of discerning the beauty of my situation. But you kept me from that fate by your kind considerations and observations of life. I would have missed what it would have been like to be fragile enough that someone like Scarlett Carlyle could introduce me to the awe of life and God. Yes, God, the One who I saw as the ruler of domains confined to history or institutions. You got me to see that it was in a graveyard in Sicily, in the soul of Sandy

Templeton, in the capacity for humanity to think beyond itself, in the nobility of death beyond just sacrifice, and on the journey all of us must inevitably take to what's next.

And dare I say it? I saw God in me! The God I had confined to walls and creed suddenly exploded everywhere in my last few weeks. It was like looking through a kaleidoscope – a different burst of colour and design with every turn.

There is a school in architecture that says the ultimate goal of the designer is to create structures worthy of the spirit that will inevitably inhabit them. Yes, you use history, learned knowledge, engineering, physics, and all the rest, but such things are tools which you must utilize to build a habitat greater than the sum total of redeeming aspects of humanity. That is what you have become for me. You took St. Anne's and made it into something so much bigger and more meaningful than death, rite of passage, grief, or comfort. In fact, you turned it into a hostel – a place where travellers rest but for a night before journeying on to greater things the next day.

I was right about you from the very beginning. When I said I wanted to remain unbreakable, I could see the resolve in you to help me understand the ignorance of my ways. And you did break me – not with harsh words or guilt, but by transcending my limited world with your own. There is no guard strong enough to overcome the nobility of soul. I leave this world not as a broken man in pieces, but someone far better equipped for the next step forward. Which is where I will be when your time comes. We'll go together, you and I, just as we have for this past year. Be looking for me at that time.

Bert

P.S. You'll note that I have left you my Triumph Herald. It's all gassed up and reconditioned. I have the keys by your wine rack. You've worked so hard. You need to get out more. Take the top down and head to white cliffs. Our spirits will meet there.

THE END

ABOUT THE AUTHOR

Glen Pearson resides with his family and children in London, Ontario. He served as a professional firefighter for 30 years before becoming a Member of Parliament for London North Centre.

He has headed the London Food Bank for the past 35 years and also has helped direct the African non-governmental organization (NGO) Canadian Aid for Southern Sudan for the past 22 years. He and his wife have adopted three children from that region.

Glen is also the author of over 60 books, blogs regularly at glenpearson.ca and writes as a columnist for the London Free Press and National Newswatch.